PRAISE FOR
RHYTHM ALCHEMY

"Martin Ivanov is an enigma. He is both a scientist and a musician with a knack for deciphering ancient esoteric knowledge and distilling them into a form that is both understandable and practical for the common man. His book **Rhythm Alchemy** is one of those few rare books that I have read and wished I had come across it sooner in my Life! Most of the questions I have tackling Thracian origins and the deeper wisdom of Hermes Trismegistus have been answered by Martin through precise attention to historical and archaeological data as they relate to our understanding of Mathematics, Sacred Geometry and the Rhythms of Life itself!

If you have read my book *The Meta Secret* you MUST read this book!!! It takes you through the complexities of Ancient Secrets that Martin has so aptly deciphered and reveals to you the world around as you have never perceived it before. I highly recommend this book as one you need to keep on your shelf of important life-changing tomes!"

— DR. MEL GILL, author of *The Meta Secret: Anything is Possible*

"**Rhythm Alchemy** is a wonderful, fascinating, inspiring and complex book. First Martin Ivanov gives us a survey of the ancient wisdom and esoteric knowledge of harmonics, correspondences, rhythms and human development. Then he takes us into a practical workbook that uses the accompanying audio CD to support us in our own transformational and healing process. He concludes with heart-touching and practical examples of how this approach can be applied in a variety of settings from children with special needs through to senior management. Unique and enjoyable for anyone interested in the invisible dynamics of sound in both a personal and a cosmic context."

— WILLIAM BLOOM, author of *The Endorphin Effect* and *The Power of the New Spirituality*

RHYTHM ALCHEMY

IN SEARCH OF THE PHILOSOPHER'S STONE

MARTIN IVANOV

TRANSLATED BY
DAVID MOSSOP & MARTIN IVANOV

© Martin Ivanov, 2012, 2014

The right of Martin Ivanov to be identified as
the author of this work has been asserted by him in accordance
with the Copyright, Designs and Patents Act 1998.

Published in 2014 by Findhorn Press, Scotland

ISBN 978-1-84409-648-0

All rights reserved.

The contents of this book may not be reproduced in any form,
except for short extracts for quotation or review,
without the written permission of the publisher.

A CIP record for this title is available from the British Library.

Edited by Michael Hawkins
Illustrations: see credits page 216
Cover design by Richard Crookes
Interior design by Damian Keenan
Printed and bound in the EU

Published by

Findhorn Press

117-121 High Street,

Forres IV36 1AB,

Scotland, UK

t +44 (0)1309 690582

f +44 (0)131 777 2711

e info@findhornpress.com

www.findhornpress.com

Contents

	About the Author	7
	Foreword	9
	The Discovery	12

PART I - DISCOVERY 13

1	The Lost City of Atlantis	14
2	Megaliths	18
3	The Legacy	23
4	Toth the Atlantean	25
5	3	27
6	Toth the Atlantean goes to Egypt	29
7	The Great Pyramid	31
8	Hermes Trismegistus and Hermetic Philosophy	34
9	Orpheus	37

PART II - TRUTH AND RHYTHM 39

10	The Beginning	40
11	Maya	42
12	Vibration	45
13	Rhythm	48
14	The Door	51
15	The Key	55
16	1 366 560	60
17	Pythagoras	64
18	Tetractys and the 47th Theorem	68
19	The Threefold Law	71
20	Microcosm and Macrocosm	79
21	Rhythm and Tetractys	82
22	13	86
23	The Evolution of Consciousness	91
24	Rhythm and Polyrhythm	96

PART III - ALCHEMY — 99

25	The Capstone	100
26	Alchemy and the Philosopher's Stone	104
27	Mental Transmutation	106
28	From Aristotle to Geber	109
29	The Initiation Process	114
30	The Tablet of Isis	118
31	9	123
32	The Matrix of the Capstone	125
33	3 x 3 x 3 (length)	127
34	13 (width)	132
35	The Virtual Interactive Matrix	136
36	Cause and Effect – 1st level	143
37	Correlation – 2nd level	147
38	Finding Your Way	152
39	Tuning the "strings" – 3rd level	157
40	Mental Transmutation – 4th level	161
41	Induction	166
42	Telepathy	169

PART IV - ANCIENT MUSIC — 173

43	Ancient Music	174
44	The Ancient Alchemical Instrument	177
45	Restrictive Beliefs and Convictions	180
46	Rhythm Session in Prison	183
47	Corporate Rhythm	186
48	Rhythm and Autism	190
49	The Old Man and the Drums	194
50	The Children from Doganovo	198
51	Rhythmology	205
52	The Rhythmology Experiment	207
53	Conclusion	209

Illustration Credits	216
Bibliography	217

About the Author

Martin Ivanov is a Bulgarian composer, conductor and percussionist who spent 15 years in the USA and Canada following his calling. He graduated from the prestigious Berklee College of Music, Boston (jazz composition and arranging / summa cum laude), University of Memphis and the University of Massachusetts (MA and Ph.D. degrees in fine arts and composition), Sofia University "St. Kliment Ohridski" (Master of Business Administration).

From 2001 to 2004 Martin taught composition, harmony, arranging and jazz ensembles at the University of Memphis and University of Massachusetts. He has performed and composed for internationally acclaimed artists and orchestras. Having gained invaluable experience abroad he has now returned to his home country to devote his talents and experience to create something indispensable.

On returning to Bulgaria, he founded the Institute of Contemporary Art and Therapy "Libera". His primary motivation was to use his creative knowledge to create and develop social projects, therapies and to train other people.

Martin is the founder of drum / rhythm therapy and facilitation in Bulgaria. He has created many programmes including: Rhythmology, Art Rhythm, Corporate Rhythm, Happy Drum (Rhythmology for children), Rhythm Relax. He has organized many rhythm-based social, educational, corporate and therapeutic events based on rhythm, using a wide range of percussion instruments.

The positive vibrations of his drums attempt to respond to cries for help and address the need for social support in prisons, psychiatric hospitals, nursing homes, orphanages, day care centres for children with disabilities, and oncology clinics. Martin's corporate rhythm-based trainings have proved very popular. Clients include global companies such as Microsoft, AVON, HP, Citibank, Shell, Deloitte, Nestlé, Heineken, Carlsberg, Renault Nissan, VMWare, SAP Labs, Bayer, and Konica Minolta.

Martin Ivanov is a passionate motivational speaker and he uses the language of rhythm as a tool for personal and collective development. He is frequently interviewed on radio and television.

Foreword

I spend a lot of time thinking about how we look at composition as the process of creating music. Isn't there a creative process connected to just about anything? Yes, composing a musical piece is creative, as is drawing a picture, sculpting a figure, writing a poem, choreographing dance. They are all creative processes and none is greater than the composition of my life… your life.

Composition is creation. Composition is the creator's ability to work freely with the language of his chosen form. The skill of the composer lies in his unique knowledge, experience and ability to make the right choices. The quality of the composition is determined firstly by the impact on the people whom it is meant to influence, and secondly the satisfaction which the creator receives from bringing it to life.

In addition to the physical and motor skills required to perform his composition, the composer has to find the spiritual and emotional resources required to bring light to his career. The composer must have the right creative vehicle and performance space, if he wants to achieve his compositional plan. Put in other words – this is the language in which the composer creates.

The musical composer has his score, the artist has his canvas, the sculptor has his stone, the writer has his sheet of paper, the actor and the dancer have their stage. The simple sheet music becomes a score when the physical presence of the notes is interwoven with spiritual and emotional decisions in such a way that it delivers the creator's idea and his feelings and sends his message to the performer and listener.

What determines the physical quality of a musical composition? The answer to this question is pure and simple. The notes are written on the page and you play them in the way they're written. The sound which is produced is defined by the motor activity needed to reproduce the sounds generated.

What determines the spiritual and emotional quality of a musical composition? These are the subtleties noticed by the sensitive observer such as orchestration, duration, energy, main tempo, development of basic idea, dramatic events, tension and release patterns, climax points, etc. Without the spiritual factor, the musical notes would exist in space devoid of any sense, character, value and purpose.

Can an analogy be made between the composition of music and the composition of our lives? If the creator of the Cosmic Symphony, which defines our time and existence, created a score which must be interpreted, what is it? What are its spiritual and physical parameters? What is our role as co-creators and performers in this cosmic orchestra? How do we follow the conductor if we want to perform a meaningful composition of our lives? What knowledge do we need to participate actively in the creation of this work?

Rhythm Alchemy provides us with the spiritual and physical parameters of our cosmic score. It will guide us to our place in the composition and provide us with the ideas and knowledge we need to participate fully in both – how to compose our life and fulfil our innermost dreams.

Music composition uses the language of rhythm, melody and harmony. In my review of the Cosmic Score I will work with rhythm since it is the basis from where melody and harmony are derived. You might doubt the validity of my statement and this is understandable. We all take pleasant melodies and harmonies for granted, even though they are an intricate combination of tones played either individually or in unison.

When we play or sing notes of varying pitch successively we create a melody which moves horizontally in a linear fashion. Harmony, however, is born out of the vertical interrelation between the tones of several melodies. So how exactly are these tones created?

Each tone is a sound vibration – a sequence of motion and stillness, sound and silence. It is a cyclical pattern of two phenomena which, per se, is rhythm. The pitch of the tone is created by rhythmic oscillation at a precise frequency. If the frequency of the vibration is slow, the tone will be lower in pitch. Conversely, if the frequency is fast, the tone will be higher in pitch. Frequency is measured in Hz. Thus the different tones/notes which form the building blocks of the melody, and the harmony, are no more than the rhythms in space resounding at varying vibration speeds.

We may not realize how often we use musical terms like rhythm, melody and harmony to refer to things which happen to us in our daily lives. For example, the rhythm of our heart and how our feelings soar in space; the melody of our personal inner voice trying to interweave with the harmony of other voices around us. We are constantly seeking and wanting to write the composition of our "Happiness".

When we compose this work, even though we tirelessly seek inspiration from outside us, our score often remains blank. This is because we do not pay sufficient attention to the true inspiration which lies within us. In order to reach this inspiration, we need to rebuild the bridges linking us to the roots of our true nature – rhythm.

When we begin the intimate dance with the vibrations of our existence and begin to experience the real flavour of each wave which colours our emotions, then we will attain the creative power of the composer expressed in what we call "happiness".

— Martin Ivanov, Sofia, Bulgaria, 2012

The Discovery

*Under, and back of, the Universe of Time,
Space and Change, is ever to be found,
The Substantial Reality – The Fundamental Truth.*

— *THE KYBALION* [1]

In 1952 Alberto Ruz Lhuillier[2] made the most significant archaeological discovery in Mexico of all time. After three years of agonizing digging, his team cleared the gravel-filled staircase leading down into the Temple of the Inscriptions in the ancient Mayan city of Palenque. Finally they reached a massive triangular solid plate used to close the entrance. Behind that triangular door, Alberto Ruz Lhuillier discovered the revelation of a secret message to all of humanity today – *The Fundamental Truth*.

---

1 *The Kybalion* – Hermetic philosophy, reflecting the essence of the teachings of Hermes Trismegistus. The book was published anonymously in 1908 under the name *Three Initiates*.

2 Alberto Ruz Lhuillier (1906 – 1979) – Mexican archaeologist. He specialized in pre-Columbian Mesoamerican archaeology and is well known for leading the National Institute of Anthropology and History (INAH) excavations at the Maya site of Palenque, where he found the tomb of the Maya ruler, Pakal. Ruz Lhuillier is sometimes referred to as the *"Hitchcock of Archaeology"*.

PART I

Discovery

ONE

The Lost City of Atlantis

*Time reveals everything hidden and
conceals everything which is clear.*
— SOPHOCLES

Our adventure begins in Atlantis, the mythical continent hidden beneath the waves of the Atlantic. Although there has never been any proof of its actual existence, much evidence has come to light over the years suggesting the might of its domain.

The city of Atlantis was eulogised in the works of Plato and other classical authors. The civilization of Atlantis flourished for more than 13,000 years only to be destroyed overnight by a global disaster. About 12,500 years ago an increase in solar activity led to a dramatic increase in global temperatures. Glacial ice melted and the level of the oceans increased by 130 metres. Atlantis disappeared in the catastrophic floods at the end of an era aligned with the sign of Virgo.

Most of the information we have about Atlantis has come to us through historical or psychic sources.

The oldest historical description of the sunken continent comes from 360 BC, through the works of Plato, in particular the dialogues of "Timaeus" and "Critias". According to Plato what is known about Atlantis was told to Solon, an Athenian legislator, by the oracles from the Egyptian city of Sais. Solon spent about ten years in Egypt in about 600 BC. He then recounted the story to Dropides, a relative of his, who then in turn told his son, Critias. Critias the elder, while he was still young, passed the story down to his nine-year-old grandson with the same name. In both dialogues, Critias the younger takes the role of narrator recounting the story of Atlantis.

In addition to Plato's accounts, the folklore of the Greeks, Irish, Egyptians, African, Northern Europeans, Mesopotamians and Andeans also preserves tales about an ancient civilization, the centre of which was located on a large island in the middle of the Atlantic.

In the same way that everyone has a personal memory, nature and the universe also retain and record all the events of the past in a collective super memory. These are the Akasha chronicles. They contain the past and present of everything and every person on the planet and the relationship between them is based on psychic connections. Exceptional individuals such as Edgar Cayce, Elena Blavatska, Charles Webster, Rudolf Steiner have obtained information about Atlantis from the Akasha chronicles and contributed information to them as well.

History textbooks tell us that man evolved from apes in Africa one million years ago, homo sapiens, or the thinking man, evolved 40,000 years ago and that the oldest civilization in the world dates from 5300 BC, in Sumeria. These same textbooks, however, give no information about what happened between the appearance of the first consciously thinking men, to the founding of Sumeria. This is a period of about 30 – 35,000 years. Apart from sparse information about cave paintings, the appearance of agriculture and metallurgy, history gives us no information or evolutionary evidence about how from nothing the Sumerians made brilliant scientific, artistic, architectural, astrological and other forms of discoveries.

The first writing system, counting system, laws, religion, copper and tin smelting for bronze, the naming of star constellations using names we still use today, are only a few of their achievements. They made an important contribution to the creation of all concepts and notions in astronomy such as poles, axis of rotation, equinox and solstice. The Sumerians began counting time on the earth and worked out that, at on two given days in the year, the sun rises in one and the same place.

They also realised that day and night are of the same duration. They discovered that the heavenly vaults rotate around a star which they called the "pole" star. They divided the heavens into twelve sectors and recorded each one perfectly. They gave names to all the stars. They discovered the relative positions of the stars, planets, moon and sun around the earth which itself rotates on an inclined axis through the heavens.

The most incredible discovery of them all was the cycle they referred to as the "Precession of Equinoxes" which covers 26,000 years, a huge length of time. The precession is created by the rotation of the entire solar system around Alcyone. (It is the brightest star in the Pleiades open cluster, which is a young cluster, aged at less than 50 million years. It is named after the mythological figure Alcyone, one of the mythological Pleiades.)

They are believed to have discovered this cycle when they noticed from a fixed observation point that every year equinox came just a little bit later, and that the total delay was equivalent to 1 degree every 72 years. By doing this, the Sumerians were able to define astral time to terrestrial time. They divided the circumference into twelve sectors; each of them equivalent to 30 degrees extrapolated into the sky, and designated them with the symbol of an animal. This was the Zodiac. Each sector was 2,160 years in duration.

How did the first civilization on the planet achieve this knowledge in such a short space of time without a wise, informed predecessor?

Sumeria, however, is not the only case where knowledge and achievements have suddenly appeared.

Prior to the 5th millennium BC, the valley of the Nile River was sparsely populated with indigenous peoples. Gradually new settlers began to establish themselves in the region. Even though the cultural achievements of these new settlers were to a large extent more advanced than the indigenous inhabitants, there was little suggestion of the future Egypt of the Pharaohs. However, this was to change drastically from the middle of the fourth millennium BC, when quite unexpectedly a large group of settlers appeared. These new settlers brought with them the marks of a highly developed civilization.

According to Professor B.Emery, one of the most eminent 20th century Egyptologists, their rapid rise to prosperity, immediately after the political unification of Egypt was due to the appearance of a new race. He called this the "dynastic race" and his theory is supported by discoveries of anatomical remains of people in the pre-dynastic burial mounds in Upper Egypt. They had large skulls and larger bodies than the local indigenous people. Professor Emery writes:

> The difference is obvious and it is impossible to believe that these people originated from the earlier settlers.

Their rapid development was made possible by a number of factors such as: improved irrigation methods, knowledge of handicrafts, replacement of simple dwellings with large temples, the construction of large-scale public buildings and palaces, the use of complex machinery such as the weavers' loom, the use of papyrus for making writing scrolls and the accelerated development of literacy.

Although the indigenous Egyptians had used rafts to navigate short distances along the Lower Nile, a 38 metre long ship was discovered buried in a pit along the southern end of the Great Pyramid. This ship is an indication of the advanced level of ship-building skills, and its high prow suggests that it was even seaworthy. Applied studies and analysis concluded that the ship was constructed in 3000 BC, or three centuries before the first Egyptian dynasty was founded. Thor Heyerdahl, the famous traveller and seafarer, believed that the "Egyptians were seafarers long before they arrived in the Nile".

As with the Sumerians, facts show that the Egyptian civilization was not a product of development, but rather it was inherited. All their achievements were extant at the beginning of their history. We should, therefore, ask ourselves the logical question whether it is possible for such a developed civilization suddenly to flourish.

TWO

Megaliths

Compared with the intelligence of early people, the intelligence of modern man is like comparing a microscope with a telescope. Modern man has narrowed his perceptions to study the miniature. Our distant ancestors expanded their perceptions to try to understand the cosmos. This explains, for example, why the Precession of Equinoxes has been known for hundreds of generations.
— COLIN WILSON [3]

The Pleistocene is a geological era which began 1,806 million years ago and ended 11,500 years ago. It experienced a number of ice ages and can be divided into the early, middle and late Pleistocene. Atlantis must have existed during the late period. Due to the climatic conditions extant during that period, this advanced civilization could only have existed in the tropical zones of the planet. This zone is between 35 degrees north and 35 degrees south of the equator.

According to Plato's descriptions Atlantis must have been somewhere in the centre of the Atlantic Ocean and the continent must have been in the most suitable place for it to flourish. Sumeria also flourished in this same belt – in the fertile valley of the river Nile between the Tigris and Euphrates of Mesopotamia. The valleys of the Indus River in India, and the Yangtze in China also possessed the conditions necessary for the development of civilization.

It is interesting to note that the most important classical cities such as Heliopolis in Egypt, Eridu in Sumeria, Persepolis in Persia, Harappa in India and Lhasa in Tibet were also situated at 30 degrees. These places most frequently provide us with proof of the existence of ancient civilizations and suggest that the people of Atlantis may very well have used their excellent shipbuilding and seafaring knowledge to visit all these places and bring their culture and knowledge.

---

[3] Colin Wilson (1931) – English writer and philosopher who described his philosophy as a "new existentialism" or "phenomenological existentialism".

This belt also provides us with shocking evidence of a huge natural disaster and the date of its occurrence. The ancient civilizations built unique monuments to record the date of the great flood. Since ancient times people have seen shapes in the stars. They gave names to these constellations, such as Aries or Orion the Hunter. Different ancient societies saw different animals and objects in the stars. The models of the constellations have not changed, but the precise angle of groups of stars in relation to the horizon alters over time. This is due to the "Precession of the Equinoxes", in which the Earth rotates around its axis once every 24 hours.

The earth's axis, however, has a slow tilt, rotating once every 26,000 years. The precession slowly alters our perception of the stars, and their position in the sky is unique during different moments in time. Astronomers using an astronomical computer programme have calculated the slowly changing positions of the stars over time. In fact some of the wonders of the Ancient World resemble the constellation of the stars at a precise moment in the past. In other words if they are looked at from above, the groups of monuments reflect the unique position of the stars, as they were at that precise moment in history.

Egyptologists believe that the three pyramids which were built 4,500 years ago at Giza, near modern Cairo, were purely burial tombs without any other functions. They were believed to have been constructed to provide a final resting place for the three Pharaohs of the Fourth Dynasty – Cheops, Khafra and Menkaure. However, is this the case?

The three Giza pyramids have always been surrounded by mystery. When looked at from above, you can see two large pyramids, almost identical in size, positioned diagonally in relation to each other. The third pyramid, that of Menkaure, is slightly to the east of this diagonal line. Many questions have been asked about this curious imperfection.

Orion's belt, in the middle of this constellation, is made of three stars. They also form a diagonal line with one star slightly out of line. The stars are an identical mirror image of the pyramids on the ground: two big, bright stars with a third above them, paler and slightly inclined towards the east. The smallest star deviates from the line which connects the other two by 54 degrees. The smallest pyramid, however, deviates from the line which connects the other two by 45 degrees. Here we see yet another coincidence. The difference is 9 degrees. At the moment the Great Pyramid is exactly 9 metres lower than when it was built.

As a result of the Precession, the angle of the three stars changes over time and the best coincidence occurs on a specific date. The sky moves over an unmoving earth upon which the pyramids stand. If we were to alter the sky in time to find a coincidence between the model of Orion and the pyramids, we see that this occurred in 12,500 BC. The pyramids are at a precise angle of 45 degrees to the North-South line. The three stars form this precise angle on only one date – in 12,500 BC.

This would mean, therefore, that from an architectural, symbolical and astronomical point of view the pyramids were constructed to commemorate an earlier era and that the ancient Egyptian civilization was inherited from a lost race.

A similar example can be seen in the temples of Ankor Wat in Cambodia. The temples were built by the Khmers 3,000 years after the Giza pyramids. There is a striking resemblance between the design of a number of temples on the ground and the pattern of stars in the Draco constellation, which is one of the large northern constellations. The Ankor temples appear to be a true mirror of the stars in the constellation, but there it more to it than this. Using the Precession as a basis for calculation, the Ankor Wat temples area also linked with the same date of the natural disaster. The coincidence between the monuments and the Draco constellation, also occurs only once – 12,500 BC.

14 km from Lake Titicaca, high in the Bolivian Andes, lie the ruins of one of the most enigmatic cities in the world – Tiwanaku. It is believed by archaeologists to have been the capital city of an ancient South American Empire which began to flourish about 2,000 years ago. However, the identity of Tiwanaku's founders remains a mystery. They were excellent stone masons and the temples and monuments they created consisted of huge but delicately carved, sculpted and precisely fitting stone blocks. For more than one hundred years, Tiwanaku gave rise to all manner of fantastic explanations of its origins.

As far as who built it is concerned, they might be the survivors of a lost civilization who migrated to the mountains to create a new settlement while trying to preserve their culture, traditions and religious ideas. The construction technology used in Puma Puncu, a part of this monumental complex, is even more stunning. Metal connectors were used to link the enormous stone blocks. To make this possible the builders would have needed access to a mobile furnace and such technology does not even exist today.

According to Arthur Poznansky who spent 50 years studying the site, Tiwanaku was an ancient astronomical observatory and the cradle of an ancient American civilization. He was convinced that certain stone blocks were positioned in such a way as to align with the Sun at the summer and winter solstices.

In a similar way to the constellations, the position of the solstices also changes slowly over time and Poznansky discovered the perfect coincidence between the stone blocks and the rising sun at a date 12,000 years ago. He made a very well-argued statement that the original arrangement of Tiwanaku had been designed at a time when the point of Sunrise was significantly different from the current point of the winter and summer solstice – approximately 12,000 years ago.

The huge stones, also referred to as megaliths, are particularly interesting. These stone blocks were hewn and moved over huge distances and then assembled with incredible precision. All this was achieved using technology which is unknown today. Even nowadays there is no machinery capable of lifting such blocks, let alone arrange them with such precision.

The oldest descriptions of huge stone blocks were discovered in ancient texts from Baalbek, in the Lebanon, between the Litani and Oront rivers in the fertile Beqaa valley. They refer to three cut stone blocks, which are the biggest and heaviest known in history. They are called the trilithons and consist of a huge stone platform the sides of which are 700 metres long. It was built to withstand huge weight and pressure. Each one of the three blocks weighs 1,200 tons, is 25 metres long, 8.5m high.

They were placed at a height of 8 metres upon other stones and so precisely interlinked that not even a sheet of paper can be placed between them. They were transported to the site from the place where they were hewn – 3 km away. A number of different temples were built on the platform. The oldest was built by the Sumerians, the next by the Assyrians. Another temple was constructed by the Persians who worshipped the god Mythra, who gave light. Finally there is a Greek temple. In 63 BC, the Romans conquered this incredible place and built their own temple to Jupiter.

Stonehenge in England is another megalithic monument consisting of big stone blocks arranged in a circle. In total there are about 30 blocks, the average height and weight of which is 4.5m and 25 tons. The monument has attracted the attention of many researchers. They have discovered that it was constructed in three stages. Many sources believe that the first stage of construction took place 2800 BC. In other words it dates back more than 5,000 years.

Evidence from historical sources shows that a small circle of giant stones was initially built after which a pointed "heel stone" was erected outside the circle. Later on a second circle was built from other huge stones. Then, inside these two circles, other stone blocks known as "blue stones" were erected.

Other famous ancient megalithic complexes and monuments include the Giza pyramids, Newgrange near Dublin and the wall in the ancient Inca city of Saksaywaman, near Cusco in Peru. They all provide evidence of construction technology and applied crafts which cannot be explained today. One popular theory is that the ancients discovered technology to move these huge stones by making them lighter. This technology involved the emission of sound vibrations.

In addition to the theory that Atlantis may have sunk into the depths of the ocean about 12,500 years ago, there are many other theories. One of the most interesting is that of Frank Joseph, a travel journalist who believes that Atlantis may have perished only 3,200 years ago and that it may have suffered not one, but four separate natural disasters, centuries apart. The last of these would have brought the end of the civilization.

These enormous Bronze Age cataclysms would have been caused by the proximity to the Earth or direct collision with four separate comets: Haley's Comet, Proto-Encke or Oljato comet, Hale-Bopp and Encke. These cosmic collisions would have had a fatal significance for civilization on any of the following dates: 3113, 2193, 1628 and 1198 BC.

After 3100 BC., the spiritual and material culture of the countries of Asia Minor, Middle East, Egyptian basic and the Middle East experienced extraordinary prosperity for more than two millennia. However, in approximately 1200 BC., literature, art, monumental construction, city building, medicine, religious institutions, mathematical sciences, manufacturing, physics, astronomy, trade and all the other facets of a highly developed civilization seemed to disappear overnight.

Pre-classical civilization went into irreversible decline – from pharaonic Egypt and Homeric Greece to the Hittite Empire and the Chinese Shin Dynasty. Atlantis was only one of the victims of the global catastrophe. Just like all the others it was part of the Bronze era civilizations.

These events are described in the myths and legends of Egypt, Mesopotamia, Morocco, the Canary Islands, Ireland, Wales, Scandinavia, Pre-Columbian North America, Mesoamerica and South America before the Spanish conquest.

THREE

The Legacy

Papyri burn; words carved in stone erode; clay tablets crumble. But a vitally important message wrapped in myth endures over time like the body of an insect preserved in amber.
— FRANK JOSEPH

How and when Atlantis perished is not relevant to the purpose of this book. However, my purpose is to draw your attention to the existence of this highly developed civilization which has left us the seeds of crucial knowledge. During the *"evolution"* of our humanity, we have lost faith in the stories, legends and myths that connect us directly to this ancient wisdom. We have let our five senses dictate our perception of the world and the reality which surrounds us. Truth and real knowledge have become hidden beneath the veil of all our limited belief in reality.

It may now be time to uncover and develop something that we all possess, but only a few of us can really use. That something is our intuition – the sixth sense which the ancient Atlanteans used to understand the universe and develop their invaluable wisdom. As Vaclav Havel, the former president of the Czech Republic says:

> We may know more about the universe than our ancestors did, and yet it seems they knew something more essential about it than we do.

Ancient civilizations are believed to have left us a legacy of great mysteries. These secrets have been cleverly encoded in numbers, symbols, monuments, books and stories. The universal key to unlock the holy mystery of life was hidden in these important messages. The messages themselves were hidden because in the hands of ignorant, cruel, power-hungry people, the secrets could lead to the end of humanity.

Matthew 7:6:
…Do not give dogs what is holy, and do not throw your pearls before pigs, lest they trample them underfoot and turn to attack you.

In his book *Everyone is Right*, Roland Peterson concludes:

Some knowledge in the hands of morally unprepared people can be devastating for themselves and the others.

This is the main reason these secrets were passed encrypted from one generation to another. In actual fact this information has always been around us and accessible to everyone. If you want to conceal something well, you put it somewhere in full view. When our senses perceive something as a reality and we take it for granted, it is difficult to look at it in another way and see the truth. For example, we are so used to the feeling that our physical body is solid material, that the idea it might be just simple vibrations sounds insane. There is an old hermetic axiom which says:

When the ears of the student are ready to hear, then cometh the lips to fill them with wisdom.

To get to the heart of the truth and look beyond the horizon of our limited vision, we have to break down the barriers of our mind and open our senses to new perceptions. We need to delve into the myth of Atlantis and accept the mysterious clues left to us by history. Atlantis has left us its wonderful legacy, and we can perceive it by trusting to our intuition and opening our ears to ancient wisdom. Sooner or later, the thirst for knowledge and the relentless search for the truth about ourselves and the world will take us to the gates of this mythical continent.

FOUR

Toth the Atlantean

Long time ago, I in my childhood, lay 'neath the stars on long-buried ATLANTIS, dreaming of mysteries far above men. Then in my heart grew there a great longing to conquer the pathway that led to the stars. Year after year, I sought after wisdom, seeking new knowledge, following the way, until at last my SOUL, in great travail, broke from its bondage and bounded away. Free was I from the bondage of earth-men. Free from the body, I flashed through the night. Unlocked at last for me was the star-space. Free was I from the bondage of night. Now to the end of space sought I wisdom, far beyond knowledge of finite man. Far into space, my SOUL travelled freely into infinity's circle of light.

— TOTH THE ATLANTEAN

This is how Toth, the oracle and King of Atlanta, described his childhood in *The Emerald Tablets*[4].

He grew to manhood under the guidance and advice of his father, Tothmes, who was the supreme oracle and one of the three great Atlantean teachers who gifted light and knowledge to their people.

Toth also wanted to become a teacher of people and to lead them in the search for light. He wanted to release them from the veils of the night and lead them along the path of sacred knowledge and so he studied the secrets preserved in the secret archives of the Temple. His abilities and skills grew with every passing day and he quickly learnt all the truths as they were revealed to him.

Enlightened by the fire of great knowledge, Toth's living force became much stronger than that of the ordinary people. He acquired power over life and death

---

[4] *"The Emerald Tablets"* is a text which is claimed to belong to Toth – Hermes Trismegistus and is believed to reveal the secret of the primary substance and its transmutations. The quotes used in this book are taken from the *"Emerald Tablets of Toth Atlanta"* which gives a detailed *"interpretation"* of the original tablets.

and developed the ability to leave his own body and travel at will to the most distant reaches of time and space.

Nourished by the wisdom of the cosmos, he realised that wisdom is concealed in the hearts and minds of people and that the cosmos expands endlessly through people.

Toth teaches people that darkness is only a veil and that eternal light is sealed in their hearts. It is only waiting to be released. Freedom can only be achieved through wisdom. Knowledge brings wisdom and wisdom is strength. Wisdom leads us to the knowledge that everyone is part of one All, which is greater than everything we know. Everything which exists, originates from the light, and the light originates from the All. Every person needs to aim for perfection in order to achieve personal goals. Even though nothing is perfect, perfection needs to be the main aim and ambition, since light comes to those who make the effort.

Toth believed that everything which has been created is based on a specific order. This order originates from the law which rules the cosmos where infinity reigns. The great cycles are born out of equilibrium and move harmoniously, while time and space move in cycles. With the knowledge of this law, everyone can achieve freedom.

The ancient King of Atlantis was convinced that by creating the song of the soul and generating positive vibrations, people can achieve oneness with the All. He believed man to comprise only the soul and that the body was nothing. The soul is everything and the body must not be allowed to create fetters for it, since you cannot live when you are captivated by your body. He believed that only the soul is free in space and it really does possess life. Everything else is but captivity and fetters from which man must be freed.

Toth warns of the chaos in life and the need for it to be balanced and ordered. He appeals for the need to bring order to the chaos of feelings. The forms and convictions which people create when they appear in their conscious mind are consequences of their reasons. Everything which exists is another form of something which does not exist. Every life passes into another life, and man is no exception. Death comes but does not remain forever, because eternal life exists in everything. It is but an obstacle on the way, quickly vanquished by the infinite light.

Toth teaches that the door to life passes through death. The heart is the root of knowledge and within it a secret is concealed. The secret is the source of all life and the source of all death. Thus thoughts need to be directed inwards, not outwards.

FIVE

3

Find in the keys of the numbers I bring thee, light on the pathway from life unto life. Think of the numbers that lead thee to Life
— *TOTH THE ATLANTEAN*

Toth's overriding desire to achieve wisdom and gain access to the secrets of life and the universe led him to the mystery of the great *THREE*. In prehistory there are three unities. Anything differing from them could not exist. These unities were the balance and source of creation: one God, one truth and one freedom.

Three come forth from the three of the balance: all life, all good, all power.

Three are the qualities of God in his Light-home: Infinite power, Infinite Wisdom, Infinite Love.

Three are the powers given to the Masters: To transmute evil, assist good, use discrimination.

Three are the things inevitable for God to perform: Manifest power, wisdom and love.

Three are the powers creating all things: Divine Love possessed of perfect knowledge, Divine Wisdom knowing all possible means, Divine Power possessed by the joint will of Divine Love and Wisdom.

Three are the circles (states) of existence: The circle of Light where dwells nothing but God, and only God can traverse it; the circle of Chaos where all things by nature arise from death; the circle of Awareness where all things spring from life.

All things animate are of three states of existence: chaos or death, liberty in humanity and felicity of Heaven.

Three necessities control all things: beginning in the Great Deep, the circle of Chaos, plenitude in Heaven.

Three are the paths of the Soul: Man, Liberty, Light.

Three are the hindrances: lack of endeavour to obtain knowledge; non-attachment to god; attachment to evil. In man, the three are manifest.

Three are the Kings of power within.

Three are the chambers of the mysteries, found yet not found in the body of man.

SIX

Toth the Atlantean goes to Egypt

Age after age shall ye live through your wisdom, Aye, when o'er Atlantis the ocean waves roll, holding the Light, though hidden in darkness, ready to come when e'er thou shalt call.
— THE EMERALD TABLETS

At a fatal moment for Atlantis, Toth was chosen by his teacher to be the ambassador of Atlantean culture and wisdom. He gathered the remaining sons of Atlanta after the great flood and set off for the lands of long-haired barbarians. They lived in caves in deserts in the land of Khem[5]. Those who travelled with him were not ordinary people but learned men, philosophers and clerics.

In addition to his wisdom, Toth took with him all his manuscripts. His instructions were that they be preserved until a time when people would be ready to accept their wisdom. His personal mission, engraved upon his mind, is expressed in the words he uttered when he left great Atlantis:

> You must be the light over the ages, hidden but revealed to the enlightened.

The surviving Atlanteans were met by the people of Khem with sticks, spears and growing anger. Toth retaliated with his staff. He stunned them with a wave of vibrations and then spoke to them with peaceful and reassuring words. He told them of the power of Atlantis and that they were messengers bearing new knowledge. He captivated them with its magical science and won their respect and trust.

The teachings of the Atlanteans found fertile soil in the lands of ancient Egypt first of all. They spent a long time in the Egyptian lands and Toth achieved great deeds, helping people to acquire knowledge. Their nation became great and powerful. They conquered the peoples around them and the strength of their souls slowly began to grow. The time came eventually when Toth had to obey his teacher's in-

---
5 Khem is the Arab name for Egypt

structions to spread the sons of Atlantis in many directions, in order that *"from the womb of time, wisdom might blossom in their children"*. Egypt became the centre of the new race of wisdom.

Due to his wisdom and radiance, Toth gradually began to be accepted by the Egyptians as a divinity. He is believed to be the founder of alchemy and one of the most ancient and mysterious divinities in Western Egypt. He was revered by the ancient Egyptians as the founder of the sciences and the arts, inventor of literacy and the archivist of the underworld, as well as the patron of libraries.

In art, Toth is usually depicted with the head of an Ibis (the beak of which resembles the new moon) and moon-shaped sickle above it depicting wisdom. Sometimes he is depicted with the face of a peacock and the body of a man, or entirely as a peacock, the symbol of the evolution of man in time.

Some of Toth's names include:

> *"The counter of time and the seasons", "He who counts the sky, stars and the Earth", "The God of Balance", and "The Master of Balance", "The Master of the Divine Body", "He who has achieved everything beneath the Heavens".*

SEVEN

The Great Pyramid

*Builded I the Great Pyramid, patterned after the pyramid of
Earth force, burning eternally so that it, too, might remain
through the ages. In it, I builded my knowledge of "Magic-Science"
so that I might be here when again I return from Amenti.*

— TOTH

In the chapter about Megaliths we did not discuss in great detail the greatest and most enigmatic structure in the world. In this chapter I intend to pay special attention to it. The Great Pyramid is close to Giza in the Nile valley in Egypt. It is the only one of the seven wonders of the ancient world which still exists. The Great Pyramid is the luminary of knowledge and its location is precise from both an astronomical and geographic sense.

Herodotus, considered by many to be the "father of history", believed that the Great Pyramid was the tomb of the Pharaoh Cheops. This led to a common belief which has not been proven. The burial chamber was never completed although according to all the rules of pyramid construction it should have been built at the same time as the rest of the monuments or soon afterwards. Nor is there any proof that the Great Pyramid was constructed by the Egyptians, since the bas-reliefs on the stone blocks in the burial chambers in the Valley of the Kings completely lack those architectural elements and decorations, in particular the inscriptions, images, cartouches [6] and other distinguishing features which are typical of Egyptian dynastical funereal art.

Toth's name is linked to the invention of scales, the water clock and the cubit unit of measurement, as well as the construction of the Great Pyramid, in which the wisdom and secret messages to future generations are encrypted. Toth the Atlantean, the architect and constructor, was later to be called Hermes Trismegistus.

---

6   Cartouche – cartouche in Egyptology is the oval which surrounds the name of the Pharaoh when it is inscribed in drawings.

He preserved the secret teachings of the Atlanteans and enabled anyone with open eyes and ears to learn the secrets. Toth's connection with the Great Pyramid is yet more confirmation of the fact that the pyramid was the primary temple of the Invisible and Supreme Deity. The Great Pyramid was not an observatory or burial chamber but the first temple of the Mysteries[7], the first building to serve as a repository for those secret truths upon which all sciences and arts are based.

The Great Pyramid was constructed upon a granite plateau where according to ancient history, the river Nile once flowed. The height of the pyramid, taking into account the cap-stone[8] when it was in place, is 148.1328m. The length of the base of each of the sides is 232.8672m and the surface area of the entire site is 13 acres (52.609 sq. m). The tip of the Great Pyramid is situated at exactly 30 degrees north, latitude, and 29 degrees, 58 minutes, 51 seconds longitude to the east of Greenwich.

Due to the displacement of continental tectonic plates 18,190 years ago, this site would have been precisely at 30 degrees, precisely oriented towards the North. thirty degrees latitude and 30 degrees longitude is the absolutely precise location and correlation between the height, the foundation and angle of the sides. The vertical cross-section represents two sacred triangles (3:4:5). If the dimensions are divided by themselves, then the number of Pi (π) is obtained – 3.14. This reveals that Toth knew about the mathematical constant π – the ratio between the length of the radius and the circle.

This knowledge is believed to have been discovered by Pythagoras much later than this. An indicator of advanced technology used in the perfect construction is the enormous dimension of the project: an artificial mountain constructed from 6,000,000 tons of stones. There were more stones than were used to construct all the cathedrals and churches throughout history. A design of such dimensions could not have been constructed even by contemporary technologists.

As far as we know, the Great Pyramid is the only one of its kind in Egypt containing internal chambers. In this way it rebuts the claim that all such pyramids are built upon an underground chamber where an Egyptian ruler was buried. The Great Pyramid contains three chambers: the Royal chamber, preceded by an anteroom, the Queen's chamber and the underground chamber.

The entire surface of the pyramid was covered by 144,000 white marble blocks, perfectly polished and cut with mathematical precision with right angles on all sides and no more than 2mm between them. For nine centuries each one of the

---

7   Mystery – Act of enlightenment in the secrets of sacred knowledge.
8   Capstone – The tip of the pyramid which represents a miniature model of the entire structure.

sides of the pyramid shone like a triangle of light in the reflected light of the sun's rays falling on the polished stones.

EIGHT

Hermes Trismegistus and Hermetic Philosophy

And they call him Three Times Great, since he was the greatest philosopher, the greatest oracle and the greatest King. Second after him amongst the ancient theologians was Orpheus. After him Aglaophemus, who was initiated by Orpheus in the secret teaching, in turn he initiated Pythagoras in theology. Then Pythagoras was collaborate with Philolaus, the teacher of our divine Plato.
— *MARSILIO FICINO* [9]

For hundreds of years Egyptian culture developed as trade and contacts with other peoples expanded. In this way much ancient Egyptian knowledge and the art of alchemy reached Greece. Gradually a collective image of the Greek god, Hermes, and Toth, – Hermes Trismegistus (from the Greek Hermes, the Three Times Great) the Egyptian deity of wisdom and literacy began to develop.

Hermes is believed to have acquired the name from the triple nature of his teaching and his triple vocation of philosopher, oracle and king. Over the years many historians, philosophers and theologians have shared a number of polarised opinions about Hermes Trismegistus. Some believed him to be the biblical prophet Enoch, while others considered him to be an ancient sage who lived during the time of Moses. Hermes Trismegistus is believed also to be the discoverer of alchemy, numbers, geometry, astronomy, letters and music.

Hermes also finds his way into the Arab world and culture and is associated with the prophet Idris. The Arab Hermes is also referred to as the Three Times Great due to his triple origin: devoted to the ancient mysteries of the secrets which

---

[9] Marsilio Ficino (1433–1499) – Italian philosopher, theologian, astrologer, one of the most influential thinkers of the Italian Renaissance. He restored the Platonic Academy and Neo-Platonism. In his ideas he tries to unite the ancient traditions of Pythagoreanism, Platonism, Neo-Platonism, and Hermeticism with Christianity.

rule the world; living in Babylon and enlightener of Pythagoras; the first man to be enlightened in the ancient science of alchemy.

Hermes Trismegistus is considered to have written a large number of texts; 42 sacred texts, most of which were destroyed when the library of Alexandria burnt down. The teachings of Hermes Trismegistus have come down to us today through a number of primary essays, such as *Corpus Hermeticum*, *Tabula Smaragdina* and *Kybalion*.

I would like to focus on the last of these three, the *Kybalion*, which is a collection of Hermetic teachings passed down from teacher to pupil through the ages. The meaning of the word *Kybalion* has been lost in time, but the original maxims, axioms and recommendations have been preserved. Furthermore, comments and analyses have been added by three anonymous "enlightened" authors.

It is believed that every age had its devotees who preserved the Hermetic tradition. These devotees passed down the ancient knowledge only to selected individuals. They knew that real knowledge can be preserved much more safely in a more perfect device such as the human memory.

Quite a good definition of Hermeticism is given by the two well-known authors, Michael Baigent and Richard Leigh:

> In general, Hermeticism is a mystical tradition, a mystical body of teachings, a mystical mode of thought. Like other such traditions, bodies of teaching and modes of thought, it repudiates simplistic belief and blind faith. It repudiates codified dogma and the interpretive necessity and authority of priests. It also refuses to accept the rational intellect as the supreme means arbiter of reality.Instead, it emphasizes and extols the mystical or numinous experience – direct and first-hand apprehension of the sacred, direct knowledge of the absolute.

At the heart of Hermeticism is the undying striving for spiritual quest and self-improvement linked with a profound study of nature and the universe. Hermetic teachings do not recognize a given nationality or religion. It is universal and can be encountered everywhere without creating religious conflicts.

Hermetic philosophy is based on the seven primary universal principles, the profound knowledge and understanding of which unlock the doors of ancient knowledge:

- **THE PRINCIPLE OF MENTALISM.**
  The ALL is the MIND; the universe is mental.

- **THE PRINCIPLE OF CORRESPONDENCE.**
  As above, so below; as below, so above.

- **THE PRINCIPLE OF VIBRATION.**
  Nothing resets; everything moves; everything vibrates.

- **THE PRINCIPLE OF POLARITY.**
  Everything is Dual; everything has poles; everything has its pair of opposites; like and unlike are the same; opposites are identical in nature, but different in degree; extremes meet; all truths are but half-truths; all paradoxes may be reconciled.

- **THE PRINCIPLE OF RHYTHM.**
  Everything flows out and in; everything has its tides; the pendulum – swing manifests in everything; the measure of swing to the right is the measure of swing to the left; rhythm compensates.

- **THE PRINCIPLE OF CAUSE AND EFFECT.**
  Every Cause has its Effect; every Effect has its Cause; everything happens according to Law; Chance is but a name for a Law not recognized; there are many planes of causation, but nothing escapes the Law.

- **THE PRINCIPLE OF GENDER.**
  Gender is in everything; everything has its Masculine and Feminine Principles; Gender manifests in all planes.

NINE

Orpheus

Man, know thyself; then thou shalt know the universe and God.
— ORPHEUS

The Seven Hermetic principles resonate through the ancient lyre of another mythical figure, Orpheus – the legendary Thracian musician, singer, poet and priest. The seven strings of his magical instrument resonate with the tones of the seven planets and create cosmic music in their vibrations and rhythms. The seven strings and the six intervals between them create the pattern of motion and rest, day and night as well as the masculine and feminine principle.

The low and high notes of Orpheus' lyre express the principle of polarity, representing The All, and the deeply hidden harmony of the Universal numbers. The sounds of his instrument fascinated men and beast, fish and birds, trees and rocks alike.

Orpheus spent many years of his life in Egypt and was initiated into the secret teachings of Hermes Trismegistus. Like Hermes Trismegistus, Orpheus was also crowned three times: in the dark kingdom of Hades; on Earth and in the Heavens. Orpheus' famous saying, *Man, know thyself; then thou shalt know the universe and God,* is another version of the hermetic axiom, *As above, so below; as below, so above.*

The universe and the signature of The Gods or God is encrypted in every one of us. By learning more about ourselves, we can rediscover the great cosmic mysteries. In the words of Orpheus, but we, the initiates, who know what is above and what is below, are the saviours of souls, the Hermes of human beings, we can clearly see the confirmation of his devotion to the Hermetic philosophy.

Nikolay Gigov, in his book, *Orpheus and Europe*, writes,

> The blessed Orpheus added to his heavenly gifts and secrets of Atlantis and Egypt in order to give them to the Rhodope Mountain and Greece.

Passing through, *"the wells of the pyramids and the tombs of Egypt,"* Orpheus acquired a huge wealth of knowledge and experience which later crystallized in his own teachings – Orphism. The basic idea of Orphism is that immortality is purified by the love of the natural world for mankind. The unique healing vibration of his lyre is created by this love. It is a holy music which can replenish every living creature with strength, faith and energy.

Many of the great Greek thinkers and philosophers were keen followers of the immortal ideas of Orpheus. Plato, Hippocrates, Socrates, Aristotle, and Euripides were among them, but perhaps his foremost disciple and successor was Pythagoras. Pythagoras created his Pythagorean School to preserve the memory and teachings of Orpheus, but I will talk more about this later. Orpheus is a key figure within the concept of this book, not only is he a link in the chain of ancient knowledge, but he achieves everything through the language of vibrations, rhythm and music. His lyre is his *"weapon"*. He believes that the world can be conquered with the gentle voice of his lyre not with the blade of a striking sword. This is the main philosophy which permeates the pages you are about to read.

PART II

Truth and Rhythm

TEN

The Beginning

Knowledge begins from miracles.
— ARISTOTLE

The mother of a close friend fell ill with a serious form of cancer. The bad news was a blow for everyone – his family and close friends. I had not seen her for a long time and I had been intending to go to see her and give her some encouragement. My friend told me that despite occasional periods of remission, she was not well.

During one such period of remission, I was sitting in their kitchen and despite her serious health problems, she was as always the perfect host. She did everything she could to make me feel at home. My own mother had died years previously from a similar illness and ever since then she had done everything she could to fill the emptiness in my life. The conversation was difficult and forced, despite my desire to bring some cheer and positivism to it. The family had done everything and was continuing to do everything to treat the illness and all conventional methods had failed.

Earlier that same day I had read the introduction to the American edition of *The Healing Power of the Drum*[10] written by Dr. Shi Hong Loh, director of the department of alternative therapy at Bon Secours New Jersey Health System. During all the years of his wide oncology practice he realized that he was surrounded by anxiety, depression, hopelessness and the fear of death, both on the part of his patients and their families as well.

Dr. Loh gradually began to realise that modern medicine was inert to the matter. This gradually led him to look for other alternatives for his patients. He believed that the main problem of modern medicine is that it only treats the physical

---

10 *"The Healing Power of the Drum"* – by American psychotherapist, Robert Laurence Friedman, a remarkable range of personal experience, charming stories and captivating research which demonstrates the property of the drum to influence our health positively and favourably.

side of the human body, while the driving force – the mind, soul and spirit – is largely ignored or completely left out of "physical" medicine. Within this erroneous context, not only do we have difficulty in finding better forms of treatment for our illnesses, but we also deny the unity of our being – the body, spirit and soul.

Dr. Loh considers this a fundamental mistake of modern medicine. His oncology practice has shown him that many patients develop cancer as a result of stressful and destructive events in their lives. Many of his patients developed cancer after losing people they loved in accidents, and as a result of illness or cancer. This led him to believe that the connection between the mind and body is very fragile and an important link which affects bodily health for good and for bad.

With this thought in my mind I tried very gently to influence this connection, but I made a serious mistake. I wanted so much to be useful that I could not get the words out right and just uttered the cliché phrase, *We have to think positively*. From the look in her eyes I immediately realized that I had made a mistake. I could see her pain, anger and disgust. I was clearly just one of that group of people who could not think of anything to say and just tried the trusted recipe of positive thinking.

Unfortunately it was just like saying to an exhausted and hopeless drowning man, "There's no problem, just swim to the shore and everything will be all right!" At that moment a question came into my head, like a hammer striking a nail, "What if she hasn't the strength to think positively?" What happens if someone feels so miserable in their spirit, body and mind that they cannot make even a tiny step towards positive thinking? What happens if someone cannot imagine those exotic places, ocean waves, warm spring breeze and everything nice and positive in life, which might provide a health-giving balsam to their sensations?

I continued thinking anxiously even after I had left. Were not all these sensations just an illusion and were we not just trying to deceive something which does not exist anyway? Or rather that it exists only in our minds and not in the world outside. Is it possible to "deceive" deception itself, or to find a way to tune in to the frequency of positive vibrations, even at moments when it is difficult to think positively?

The word "illusion" flashed in front of my eyes like a traffic light and to my surprise I found myself at a crossroads, where I was waiting for the light to change to let me pass. The light changed to green and I suddenly recalled the green nephrite necklace and mask of Pakal, the great oracle who ruled the Mayans. The light let me pass to the other side.

ELEVEN

Maya

Is it possible that what the mystics have been saying for centuries is true, reality is Maya, an illusion, and what is out there is really a vast resonating symphony of wave forms that is transformed into the world as we know it only after it enters our sense?
— KARL PRIBRAM [11]

I realized that in Sanskrit the word "Maya" means illusion or deception, but it does in fact have many more meanings. The etymology of the word "Maya" was studied by Joseph Campbell, one of the greatest researchers of mythology in the 20th century. He concluded that it came from the verb "ma" meaning "give shape, form, or build". In other words it reflects the ability of the gods to change shapes, create worlds and to take on other images and masks.

Furthermore Maya means magic, optical illusion. In military terminology it means disguise or deceptive tactics. Finally from a philosophical point of view Maya means the deception of thought with regard to reality when the conscious mind perceives only a layer of deceptive reality imposed upon actual reality.

David Bohm, one of the most respected quantum physicists, believes that the perceived reality of our daily lives is in fact a type of illusion similar to a holographic image. He and Karl Pribram, the neurophysiologist from Stanford, are the main architects of the idea that our world and everything within it are an enormous hologram. In other words everything from the snowflakes to the trees, from the shooting stars to electrons are only phantom images or projection of a level of reality which is so far beyond our perception of it that it is literally beyond time and space.

Pribram believes that the objective world does not exist, at least in the way in which we are accustomed to perceiving it. What actually exists beyond us is an

---

[11] Karl Pribram (1919) – A famous neurophysiologist from Stanford University, author of the classical, neuropsychological guide, *"Languages of the Brain"*.

infinite ocean of waves and frequencies. Reality appears real to us only because our brains are capable of accepting this holographic fog and turning it into trees, stones and other familiar objects which form our world. Is it possible for reality to be a realm of vibrations and frequencies, and our brain is a type of lens which transforms these frequencies into the objective world of phenomena?

Being children of materialism and materialistic science, it is very difficult for us to accept this paradigm. For more than 400 years the scientific world has led us to the conviction that the universe represents a mechanical system comprised of stable elemental "building blocks" and reality is that which is measurable and perceivable by our five senses.

The problem of modern medicine is also based in the connection between the mind and the body, in the materialistic teaching that the only valid approach to the acquisition of knowledge is to reject all feelings and subjectivity and to be completely rational and objective. This attitude to the world treats the mind and the body as separate units and divides their essence. Moreover, it declares feelings, thoughts, emotions, intuition and imagination to be worthless.

The most serious problem of the materialistic model, however, is that it has done nothing to free human life from suffering, poverty, illness and injustice. On the contrary, year after year these problems have become exacerbated and grown like a tumour in the organism of our planet.

I decided to share these thoughts with a friend who although he considered himself as having a high level of intellect was profoundly involved in the material world. I went to his office where I knew I would find him at this time of day. I explained everything to him with great enthusiasm and he listened to me carefully. When I had finished there was an awkward silence. Kiril eventually broke the ice and looked into my eyes inquisitively, saying,

"What do you mean then? That I'm sitting here at this desk and leaning on it, but it's actually not here?"

I tried to reply, but he interrupted me.

"Or…no… wait…I'm listening to music but actually I'm not hearing anything. I'm looking at the sunset, but in actual fact it's not the sunset. I smell the scent of a nice perfume, but the scent is a deception and doesn't actually exist… are you mad?!!!"

His emotions began to escalate and he was beginning to look really irritated.

There was another awkward silence. I said nothing because I felt guilty for making his working day even harder. Kiril said nothing but I could tell from the expression on his face that he was thinking seriously.

"All right then, even if you're right, I still want the world to be the way I know it… What good is it to me if the world is just a 'soup' of waves, frequencies, vibrations and goodness knows what else?"

These words seemed to contain the truth about our material world: "What do we get out of this, that or the other?" As Michael Talbot, the author of the *Holographic Universe* writes:

> We can actually become addicted to our beliefs and behave like desperate addicts when someone tries to take away the powerful opium of our dogma.

I did not answer Kiril's question, but asked myself, *"Really what is the benefit of knowing the holographic nature of our reality?"* The answer came from an interview given by Karl Pribram.

> It's not that the world of phenomena is harmful, not right or deceptive; it's not that there aren't objects around us at a certain level of reality. However, if you look and focus on the world with a holographic system, you will get a completely different view, a different reality. This other reality can explain things which up until now have been unexplained by science: paranormal phenomena, synchronicities, the obvious meaningful coincidence of events.

I would add that by understanding this reality, we can find the correct path to resolving our endless problems and direct ourselves to a more meaningful existence. Everyone tries to rid themselves of their problems and give meaning to their lives, but the materialistic way in which we perceive the world only increases and deepens our agony.

Long before the quantum physicists, the wise men of India knew that there is something much more important concealed behind the deceptive world of our senses. The Hindu and Buddhist prophets taught and continue to teach that the world of appearances, the world which we perceive with our senses is "maya", or an illusion, and that there is something beneath this material world, something more powerful and more fundamental.

Whether by coincidence or synchronicity, the Indian tribe which left us so many missives with their brilliant knowledge of time, vibrations and rhythm, called themselves the Mayans. Perhaps the mystical inhabitants of Mesoamerica wanted to tell us that everything around us is an illusion created within the infinite sea of vibrations.

TWELVE

Vibration

*"If they ask you, 'What is the evidence of your Father in you?'
say to them, 'It is motion and rest.'"*
— WORDS OF JESUS CHRIST TO HIS DISCIPLES,
THE GOSPEL OF THOMAS APOCRYPHA

These words by Jesus Christ wonderfully describe vibration as the signature of God. The sequential logic of movement and rest, light and dark, sound and silence contains the divine nature of the universe. Everything around us and within us is vibration. Vibrations create particles, objects, people, everything which we see or do not see in the infinite universe.

As the ancient Egyptians, the Indian Shamans and Greek philosophers said, everything is a creation of vibration. Long before Christ, the Hermetic "Principle of Vibration" was created and formulated by the masters of ancient Egypt. This principle teaches us that "everything is motion" and "everything vibrates", while the difference in the various manifestations of Matter, Soul and Spirit is based on the different levels of vibration.

For example, Matter vibrates at such a low frequency that to our perceptions it has form and solidity. On the other hand the Spirit vibrates so rapidly that it is difficult for us to see it in a material form.

The Three Initiates describe the spectrum of vibrations in the following way:

> The vibration of Spirit is at such an infinite rate of intensity and rapidity that it is practically at rest – just as a rapidly moving wheel seems to be motionless. And at the other end of the scale, there are gross forms of matter whose vibrations are so low as to seem at rest.

These millions of levels of vibrations create the world in which the particle, electron, atom and molecule are manifested in what we call life. Grouped together as a result of natural attraction, they create various forms, figures, sounds, scents and colours.

In the same way, a large number of fine and microscopic cells and organisms are formed in our blood, brain and skin and at all levels of our existence. A multitude of other living beings such as microbes and bacteria are born and live in the human body, and in the same way many other bodies live in the mental sphere such as muvacals and elementals. These are even finer organisms born of man's own thought – in the way bacteria live in his physical body, in the same way elementals live in his mental sphere.

Man frequently imagines that thoughts are lifeless, but he does not see that they are more living than the physical microbes and have their birth, childhood, youth, maturity and death. Depending on their nature, they either serve man or they harm him. The Sufi[12] create them, give them form and control them. They train and manage them throughout their entire lives. They are their army and fulfil their desires. The Hermetics on the other hand considered that an understanding of the "Principle of Vibration" and its use with the suitable formulae allowed them to control not only their own mental vibrations, but also those of other people.

What are these formulae? How can we find them? What do we have to do? These are the questions which I intend to answer in the coming chapters of the book. However, before this we need to understand that our senses, feelings, moods, emotions and thoughts vibrate in a certain rhythm. They have electrical charge and the magnetic energy thus created turns us into moving magnets. In other words we possess the ability both to emit and to receive vibration waves of the same length and frequency.

Each one of us possesses what psychologist Robert M. Andersen calls our "personal resonance", the ability to attract information attuned to our individual vibration waves. He illustrates this statement with the example of a vibrating tuning fork which will create vibrations and will resonate with another tuning fork, only if the second tuning fork has a similar structure, shape and dimension.

The above example allows us to make the following conclusion: if we project positive vibrations in our behaviour, emotions and thoughts, sooner or later we will attract positive results and conversely, if we vibrate at the frequency of negativism, we will be accompanied by negative perceptions. It has been established that when we are joyful and in a good mood, our emotions emit high frequency vibrations, while at those moments when we are experiencing anxiety, fear, depression, concern and hatred, they emit low frequency vibrations.

---

12 Sufi – Sufism was an ascetic movement in Islam in the 9th century which aimed at uncovering its hidden mystical dimensions. The followers of Sufism are referred to as Sufi or Dervish.

The concept that like vibrations attract, allows us to understand that the quality of our thoughts and our desires can take on their material form. The infinite universe is filled with energy, information, potential and endless possibilities which vibrate at a given frequency. What we need to do is to vibrate with all our being at the frequency of what we want to achieve and attract. If we want a good attitude, understanding, honesty, lightness, prosperity, we need to send such vibration signals into space.

It is important to know the reasons why we do not attain our desires and why our thoughts do not become material.

The reason is that at a conscious level we are all "vibrating" in the desired direction, while at the same time our subconscious mind is pulsating in the rhythm of fear, mistrust and doubt in ourselves and all the people around us.

My observations and conclusions about vibrations have made me think more and more about rhythm, since they are per se rhythm – the cyclical nature of motion and rest. On my mental journey I was about to make a discovery and open the door of new knowledge, but I sensed that all this needs to take place under the wing of rhythm.

THIRTEEN

Rhythm

Motion is the significance of life, and the law of motion is rhythm. Rhythm is life disguised in motion, and in every guise it seems to attract the attention of man: from a child, who is pleased with the moving of a rattle and is soothed by the swing of its cradle, to a grown person whose every game, sport and enjoyment has rhythm disguised in it in some way or another
— HAZRAT INAYAT KHAN [13]

What is rhythm? According to the *Encyclopaedia Columbia*, rhythm is the basic element in music. It is connected with time, linked to the duration of sounds and their arrangement and emphasis, whether chaotic or organised, in straight and symmetric models. The western European tact system and its notation began with the formulation of rhythmic models at the end of the 17th century.

The explanation of the word continues in the same style. It is explained from a purely musical point of view, ie., that rhythm is linked primarily with music. There is no doubt that most of us accept rhythm with its musical nuance, in the way in which it affects our mood or in the way in which we react to it with our bodies. This fact may sound strange and contradictory, since in the history of the universe and humanity, rhythm has existed in all forms long before the conscious creation and understanding of music.

What word did they use before the advent of music to refer to and designate the cyclical nature and frequency of events in ancient times? The etymology of the word "rhythm" is rooted in some of the most ancient languages: ancient Greek (ritmos) and Latin (ritmus). It is clear that in the distant past people did not have the same understanding of rhythm, which we have created over time. The word rhythm was equivalent to motion and time, while for us today the words rhythm and time have somewhat different meanings. While time is a

---

[13] Hazrat Inayat Khan (1882 – 1927) – Indian mystic, musician, poet and sufist.

phenomenon which allows mankind to register the changes in the environment and the universe, rhythm is more closely connected to music and the changes and frequencies contained therein. Is it indeed possible to merge the meaning of these two words?

Most contemporary scientific, esoteric and psychological literature views time not as a fact but rather a concept or an idea. Even quantum physicists do not use the word time. They refer to the space-time continuum. Dr. Deepak Chopra in his book, *Power, Freedom and Grace* writes:

> Time is an illusion; it is an internal dialogue which we use to explain our sense or perception of change and connection.

At the same time, in the same book and in many other works, rhythm is treated as an absolute fact. However, since it is also connected with time it should also be unreal. Thus if we as human beings are structured in such a way as to accept the space time continuum in a certain way, then is the sequence of the seasons a real phenomenon, are days and nights, high and low tides, bird and fish migration real phenomena? What is used to measure them? Who measures them? Only us as humans?

Both the cosmic and the individual reason possess conscious knowledge: ie., not only we, but the Sun, Moon, Stars, Earth, Animals, Fish, Insects and Plants think and possess awareness. If we as people have such an illusory notion of time, how do the Sun, Moon and stars influence with such great accuracy the world's oceans and create the rhythms of the high and low tides?

How does the Earth rotate at a specific speed to create a twenty-four-hour cycle of day and night we refer to as the circadian rhythm? How does the mutually interdependent rhythm of the Sun, Moon and Earth create the Lunar Rhythm which represents a cycle of 28 days? How does the grunion fish make its way to a specific place (Newport Beach, California), exactly at midnight on a precise day of the year, creating the rhythm of their migration? Is time really a fruit of our illusory notions? Clearly since all the events in the lives of planets, animals and plants happen with such precision, they must measure the rhythm of their lives using the expressive resources of time.

The clock – the main spokesperson of time – measures every second with perfect precision and gives form to time with equally spaced ticking. If time did not exist, rhythm would not exist or vice versa.

I decided to analyse this mutual interrelation visually and arrived at the following:

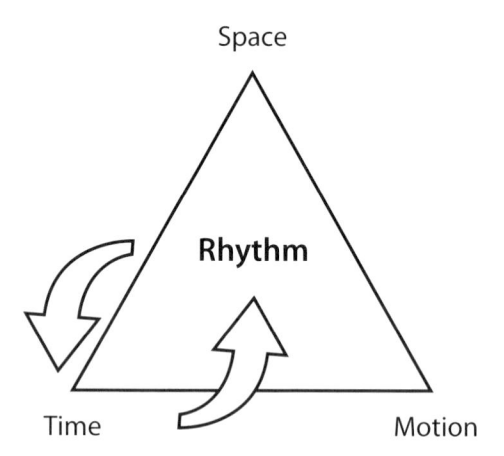

FIGURE 1

The illustration above shows the basic elements for the existence of rhythm (centre of the triangle), such as Time, Space and Motion. If we try to substitute the places of each one of the elements with that of rhythm, the only suitable association will be time-rhythm, ie., they are mutually interchangeable.

NOTE: *For this reason from here on in the book, when I refer to time I mean also rhythm and vice versa.*

FOURTEEN

The Door

Search ye the mysteries of Earth's heart. Learn of the LAW that exists, holding the stars in their balance by the force of the primordial mist. Seek ye the flame of the EARTH'S LIFE. Bathe in the glare of its flame. Follow the three-cornered pathway until thou, too, art a flame … Open the gateway within thee, and surely thou, too, shall live.
— THOTH THE ATLANTEAN

While I was working on the Rhythm triangle and defining the three factors, the words of the ancient Hermetics came into my mind:

> Beneath and beyond the World of Time, Space and Change, there is always the Substantial reality – the Fundamental truth.

I analysed these words in depth and a door to new knowledge appeared before me. This door was a triangle. It was the same door which Alberto Ruz Lhuillier had discovered in Palenque, the ancient city of the Maya. It was the door to *"Time, Space and Change"*, *"beneath and beyond"* which lies the *"fundamental truth"* – RHYTHM. *"Change"* as a factor used in Hermetic asceticism was equivalent to *"motion"* which I used in my triunity.

Of course, the door which I needed to open was different to that which Lhuillier had discovered. This door was in my mind not in Palenque. The connection I found with Alberto Ruz Lhuillier was based on the three primary "coincidences" linking my analyses, Hermetic text and the discovery made in 1952:

- Triunity and the triangular form;
- Lhuillier had discovered a massive triangular monolithic tile and what he discovered below it was *"beneath and beyond"* (see fig. 2 on the next page).

RHYTHM ALCHEMY

FIGURE 2

- *"Beneath and beyond"* the triangular door (tile) Alberto Ruz Lhuillier discovered the tomb of Pakal – the great and beloved leader of the Mayans, for whom the number 3 was the number of pulsation and the light of RHYTHM.

In the British Museum there is a skull of unknown origin given to Cortez, the Spanish conquistador by Montezuma, the Aztec ruler in the 16th century. The skull is covered with encrustations and has a triangular opening in the place of its nose:

FIGURE 3

The triangular nose symbolises the door to awareness and probably suggests that the triangular door represents much more than the treasures which Alberto Ruz Lhuillier discovered.

So what is the key to this triangular door which leads to the hidden wisdom? The "Emerald Tablets" by Toth the Atlantean contain the following:

Nine are the interlocked dimensions,

and Nine are the cycles of space.

Nine are the diffusions of consciousness,

and Nine are the worlds within worlds.

Aye, Nine are the Lords of the cycles

that come from above and below.

Space is filled with concealed ones,

for space is divided by time.

Seek ye the key to the time-space,

and ye shall unlock the gate.

Know ye that throughout the time-space

consciousness surely exists.

Though from our knowledge it is hidden,

yet still forever exists.

Clearly millennia before the so-called *"masters of time"* (the Mayans), the Atlantean Oracle leads us to one of their sacred numbers – 9 – and shows us the correct key based on time and the cycles.

While thinking about the number nines listed by Toth the Atlantean, the following table took shape in my mind:

	Interlocked dimensions	Cycles of space	Diffusions of consciousness	Worlds within worlds	Lords of the cycles
1.					
2.					
3.					
4.					
5.					
6.					
7.					
8.					
9.					

FIGURE 4

The harder I tried to complete the 45 cells with meaningful content, the more I realised that the task was beyond my abilities. This was the moment when I decided to concentrate more seriously upon the mysterious settlers of Mesoamerica.

Were the Mayans so captivated by rhythm and time that they were able to decode the ancient Atlantean wisdom and to encode it in their amazing architectural monuments? If they were, then how did they do it?

FIFTEEN

The Key

Know ye the gateway to life is through death.
— TOTH THE ATLANTEAN

Palenque is located between the mountains of the Mayans on the Pacific coast and the Yukatan (Mexico) lowlands on the coast of the Bay of Mexico. The city was a major political and religious centre with many temples. Palenque was established in 100 BC, and achieved the height of its prosperity in the 7th century and was in decline in the 9th century.

At the heart of the city state was the magnificent Temple of the Inscriptions. This was the same temple in which Alberto Ruz Lhuillier discovered Pakal's tomb. However, before we enter the temple-pyramid, we shall take a close look at the photograph to consider what it resembles.

FIGURE 5

At the top there are five entrances to the temple (horizontally) and nine levels of the pyramid (vertically). I was extremely surprised to recognize the table (fig. 4), I referred to earlier, in the Temple of the Inscriptions. Clearly this structure or form was purpose built for the content which was to be found inside it. I would like to pay particular attention to what Alberto Ruz found and to see whether it will find a place in the table.

Maurice Cotterell, who was famous for discovering the code of the Mayans, describes Ruz' discovery in his book, *The Tutankhamun Prophecies*:

> Ruz had noticed four pairs of circular holes in one of the flooring slabs of the temple at the top of the pyramid. Having scratched out the mortar filling he was able to lift the slab clear of the floor to expose a single limestone step that was covered with rumble. Brushing away the debris he came to another, and another.
>
> After 26 steps he arrived at a landing, which turned to the right to another flight of rubble-filled steps.
>
> Twenty-two steps later, three years after digging began, he was confronted by a solid limestone wall and a stone box containing eleven jade beads, three red-painted shells, three clay plates and a single pearl in a seashell filled with cinnabar, the powdered form of liquid mercury.
>
> Demolishing the wall, the excavators found themselves in a small squire chamber. Through the darkness, their flickering torches picked out the bones of one female and five male skeletons.
>
> To the left, a triangular stone door blocked the entrance to the tomb. Ruz moved the stone. For the first time in 1,250 years the tomb was opened. He was confronted by an ornately carved enormous slab of limestone measuring 3.65 metres (12 feet) long, 2.13 metres (7 feet) wide, and just under 30 centimetres (1 foot) deep, weighing around five tons. Curiously, two of the corners of the lid were missing.
>
> On 15 June Ruz descended the final four steps inside the tomb and entered the chamber. Two stone heads rested on the floor, one of which carried a 'high' hairstyle, depicting the man in the tomb.
>
> The roof of the crypt was supported by five stone beams, and nine lords of the night, as though in procession, adorned the walls. With car jacks and poles they raised the carved lid, exposing the sarcophagus below. This heavy base had one corner missing and was fastened into position with four stone plugs. Then they lifted the lid off the sarcophagus. Before them lay the bones of Lord Pacal, who died in around AD 750 at the height of Maya civilisation.

His crumbling face was covered by fragments of a jade mosaic mask. He carried a jade bead in each palm and one in his mouth. He wore four jade rings on his left hand and another four in his right, and around his neck hung a three-tiered jade necklace. By his side lay a small green jade figurine of a white man with a beard, said to be Quetzalcoatl, the feathered snake, the most revered god in Maya pantheon. The feathers represented the soaring spirit in the sky, while the snake epitomised the physical body on earth and rebirth and reincarnation, every time it shed its skin.

(from: *The Tutankhamun Prophecies*)

In the three rows of the nephrite necklace there are 3 groups of 13 beads (6+7), (6+7), (6+7), one group of 15 beads (7+8). The lowest row consists of 5 elongated beads and 4 groups of 3 round beads. If we use the Mayans' numbering system in which the dash represents 5 and the dot – 1, this gives us 8, 8, 8, 8.

Maurice Cotterell unifies all the artefacts and architectural specificities of the pyramid into a table and adds additional decryption of the calendar cycles used by the Mayans.

If we are to complete the table which I proposed with all the signs and calendar cycles decoded by Maurice Cotterell in the Temple of the Inscriptions, we arrive at fig. 6 on the following page.

RHYTHM ALCHEMY

How Maya calender cycles were encoded into the Pyramid		620 - 260 equals	Number of temple inscriptions 620 Anagram for	Sunspot cycle marker pegs on decoded tomb lid
Calendar cycles of the Maya	144,000	7,200	360	260	20

	Interlocked dimensions	Cycles of space	Diffusions of consciousness	Worlds within worlds	Lords of the cycles
	1 Pearl in seashell	1 Female skeleton in antechamber	1 Single long bead on necklace	1 Single long bead on necklace	1 Single long bead on necklace
	2 Holes in paving slab	2 Holes in paving slab	2 Holes in paving slab	2 Holes in paving slab	2 Plaster heads on tomb floor
	3 Clay plates in stone chest	3 Red shells in stone chest	3 - sided tomb drawer	3 Jade beads (1 in each hand, 1 in mouth)	3 - tiered jade necklace
Decoding the clues of the Pyramid and Temple of Inscriptions	4 Steps down into tomb	4 Jade rings on left hand	4 Jade rings on right hand	4 Set of holes in paving slab	4 Cylindrical plugs in sarcophagus
	5 Pyramid stairway landings	5 Temple doorways	5 Male skeletons	5 Ceiling beams	5 Sarcophagus sides
	6 Temple pillars	6 Sides to tomb lid	missing **6** +	missing **6** +	missing **6** +
	missing **7** +	7 Necklace beads	**7** = 13 Necklace beads	**7** = 13 Necklace beads	**7** = 13 Necklace beads
	8 = 15 Necklace beads	8 Dash-dot beads •••	8 Dash-dot beads •••	8 Dash-dot beads •••	8 Dash-dot beads •••
	9 Bottom steps of pyramid	9 Pyramid levels	9 Top steps of pyramid	9 Lords painted on tomb walls	9 Codes on left/right side of lid
Decoding in relation to calender cycles used by the Maya	9 x 144,000 +	9 x 7,200 +	9 x 360 +	9 x 260 +	9 x 20

$$= 1{,}366{,}560 \text{ days}$$

FIGURE 6

At the top of the table we see the calendar cycles of the Mayans: baktun (144, 000 days), katun (7,200 days), tun (360 days), the sacred calendar Tsolkin (260 days), unial (20 days) and kin (one day). They are encoded in the pyramid.

The first key which Cotterell discovered as he created this table was the tile with 96 hieroglyphs located in the foundations of the palace which you have to pass through before entering the Temple of the Inscriptions. These 96 inscriptions symbolise 96 micro-cycles in the 187-year cycle of the sunspots. This is a thesis which he proves in his book, *The Tutankhamun Prophecies*.

The ninety six hieroglyphs are a mirror image of the 69 steps of the Temple of the Inscriptions. The numbers are simply reversed – 96 becomes 69. Following the analogy, Cotterell arrives at the following key: the number of inscriptions in the temple – 620, an anagram of 260, an important number for the Mayans. When 260 is subtracted from 620, we arrive at 360 which is the base number of the Mayan counting system. This is what Cotterell wrote about the research process:

> I arrived at this table through mathematical inquiry into the revolutions of Venus against the base 360. The game of the Maya in the Temple was the game of numbers. All of the numbers in the table above are encoded as clues in the pyramid... At the same time, I showed how the sun-spot cycle is divided into 5 segments and these can be seen to correspond with the 5 doorways of the temple...The reason the Temple of the Inscriptions pyramid has 9 levels is to emphasize the most important number of the Maya.

Although my path to this table and Maurice Cotterell's are completely different, they have a common aim – to find the "key to time and space which will open the door" and this is the harmonious super number of the Mayans – 1, 366 560.

SIXTEEN

1 366 560

Setting these numbers down, it becomes clear just what they were trying to say: there are more 9s in the table matrix than any other number, which is not surprising, since the Maya worshiped the number 9. Taking 9 of each of the calendar cycles gives 1,366,560 days.
— MAURICE COTTERELL

Looking at the table again (fig. 6) in the previous chapter we will see that all the spaces are filled with the relevant number of signs and artefacts discovered in the Temple of the Inscriptions.

The units are represented by 3 single elongated beads in Pakal's nephrite necklace (1, 1, 1); a single female skeleton and a single pearl in a shell discovered in the urn at the base of the staircase.

The five pairs figure as 4 groups of 2 holes in the tile of the floor and 2 plaster heads discovered on the floor of the burial chamber. These heads illustrate Pakal as a young and old man. The younger figure of the ruler was carved with raised hair, as was the rule, and with two ears, while the figure of the older Pakal has only one ear. This fact will play an extremely important role in my study and we will make decisions based on this fact later in the book.

In addition to the triangular door which we have already mentioned, the series of threes is complemented by 3 serving plates, 3 shells in the stone urn, 3 nephrite beads, one in each of Pakal's hands and one in his mouth, as well as the three rows of the necklace.

Fours are represented by the 4 steps in the burial chamber, 4 rings on the right and left hand of the deceased, 4 groups of 2 holes in the floor of the burial chamber and 4 decorations in the sarcophagus.

The group of fives is formed by the 5 levels of stairs in the pyramid, 5 entrances to the temple, 5 male skeletons outside in the square chamber, 5 sides to the sarcophagus and 5 load-bearing joints in the crypt.

The group of sixes includes 6 steps of the entrance to the temple and 6 sides of the slab above the burial chamber. The remaining sixes, "666", symbolising the biblical number of the beast seem to be absent, but they can be found indirectly in connection with the sevens in the nephrite necklace.

Sevens are only to be found in the necklace as a single configuration of 7+8, four groups of one lone and three round beads, which expressed in Mayan figures means 8 8 8 8.

The last of these is a group of nines represented by the 9 levels of the pyramid, 9 lower and 9 upper steps, 9 masters on the walls and 9 codes on the lid of the burial chamber. All these signs direct our attention to the number matrix ending with the five nines, 9 9 9 9 9. When we take 9 of all the season cycles of the Mayan and 9 of the years containing 260 days, we obtain the message of the Temple of the Inscriptions: 1 366 560.

The number 1 366 560 was not discovered by Maurice Cotterell. Referred to as the "great number of synthesis" it is a sequence of fractal harmonies. It is recorded in the Dresden Codex[14] and was re-discovered by Ernst Forstman during the second half of the 19th century. This amazing number is divisible by all the key numbers of the Mayans which are linked to all the harmonious cycles. The number 1 366 560 was revered by the Mayans as the mystical "birth of the planet of Venus".

In 3113 BC, the magnetic field of the Sun reversed, suggesting that this also led to the reversal of Venus. The bright light created by this cataclysm was observed by the Mayans and accepted by them to be the birth of something new in the heavens. In fact Venus continues to rotate in the correct direction. However, due to the fact that it has been reversed, it rotates in the opposite direction to all the other planets.

This phenomenon gave rise to a new cycle of fertility, the birth of a new civilization and the appearance of a new calendar. The Mayans intensely observed and revered Venus as one of their primary deities. The morning and evening star of Venus is ineluctably linked with Quetzalcoatl – Kukulkan (for the Mayans), since he was considered to be King of the Dawn and Bearer of Light – "Morning Star".

At the same time he was also considered to be the Bringer of Death and the Guardian of the Secret Dead – "Evening Star". If from the earliest date 3113 BC., we count 1, 366 560 kins (days), or 3,796 tuns (360-day periods), we will obtain the date 631 AD. This is the golden period of the Mayans and the reign of Pakal,

---

14 Dresden Codex – With the arrival of the Spanish conquistadors in the 16th century, many of the written documents of the Mayans were destroyed or lost. Only a small number of them survived. Some of the most important manuscripts have been preserved to this day and are to be found in Dresden. They bear the name of the city where they are preserved in the Museum.

their ruler. If we calculate the divine date of the Mayans from the earliest date in units of 365 normal earth years (their Haab period), we obtain 683 AD.

It is interesting to note that from 631 to 683 AD, the year in which Pakal died and the Temple of the Inscriptions was completed, there is a period of 52 years. The cycle of 52 years is sacred for the Mayans and is directly connected with the Venus-Earth cycle of 104 years (52 + 52). It is a synchronized cycle created by the combination of the 260-day cycle Tzolkin and 365-day Haab calendars. The end and the beginning of each cycle were marked by celebratory rituals and events designating the end of the old and the beginning of the new cycle.

It is amazing how the Mayans were able to encode this number in the Temple of the Inscriptions and it is all so precisely mathematically calculated and planned in the form of numbers, signs, sculptures, drawings and architecture. No doubt many sceptics would dispute this and say that if we looked closely we could find these numbers and signs anywhere. This is what Maurice Cotterell says on this matter:

> The point is, firstly, that we have not looked very hard at all, and secondly, you will be hard pressed to duplicate this matrix using other references inside the pyramid.

Clearly this was the key I was looking for, but how could I use it? I thought I was on the right path, but this huge number frightened me from making decisions. Things needed to be simplified, but how? I eventually realized that in the process of intensive seeking, the number 1,366 560 was beginning to unlock new doors in my mind and knowledge. This key led me to Pythagorean mathematics and number teaching, in which all large numbers can be reduced and simplified to smaller numbers (from 1 – 10) by adding the integers of the number:

$$1,366\,560$$
$$1 + 3 + 6 + 6 + 5 + 6 + 0 = 27 = 2 + 7 = 9$$

Thus the great number of the Mayans is at the same time their holy number, 9.

The number of the cells in the table, (fig. 4) which represents a matrix model of the Temple of the Inscriptions, is 45. If we follow the same Pythagorean concept for number simplification, we again obtain the number 9:

$$45$$
$$4 + 5 = 9$$

Clearly the nines of Toth the Atlantean penetrated throughout the culture of the Mayans, as the primary element which defines their existence. However, let us try to reduce them and simplify them as well:

$$9 = 3^2$$

The fact that nine is equal to the number 3 squared, led me back to the number of rhythm 3, to the triangular door and to the triangle – an idea deeply rooted in Pythagorean philosophy.

SEVENTEEN

Pythagoras

*Look at the triangle and your problem is two thirds solved –
everything in nature consists of three parts.*
— PYTHAGORAS

Although Pythagoras supersedes the other Greek philosophers with his profound philosophical insights, the transcendental element of his doctrines is under-appreciated by modern materialistic science. Today the study of Pythagoras is normally limited to the Pythagorean theorem and the fact that he banned the eating of beans. All this trivialises his achievements as the first "philosopher" who laid the foundations of mathematics, mysticism and astronomy.

Pythagoras was born in 570 BC., on the island of Samos. In his early childhood he was trained in the nuances of dialecticism, physics and theogony. He studied music, drawing and athletics. At the age of 15 he was initiated into the secrets of Orphism by Aglaophamus the oracle. Pythagorean theory about the digital nature of the gods is considered to have been taken from the teaching of Orpheus. After spending seven years in Phoenicia where he studied Phoenician arithmetic and number theory, he underwent initiation in almost all the Phoenician mysteries. Pythagoras then went to Egypt.

Over a period of twelve years, from 539-527 BC, he visited all the temples in Egypt. He spent most of his time in Memphis, Hermopolis, Heliopolis, Sais and Tiva, where he was taught intensively by the Egyptian oracles. Impressed by their knowledge and spiritual energy, he began to imitate the secret symbolism which they used, and began to conceal his own teachings in metaphors.

Pythagoras so impressed the Egyptian oracles with his insatiable desire for knowledge that they allowed him to attend the sacrifices and religious services, to which foreigners had never been allowed. He observed the celestial sky, studied geometry and was given access to the secrets of the Egyptian deities.

His last journey, which led to capture by Persian soldiers, brought him to Babylon, where he came across the oracles of the supreme haldeic deity Bel Marduk. Here Pythagoras met Zoroaster,[15] from whom he acquired much valuable knowledge. Finally passing through Media and Persia, Pythagoras headed towards Hindustan, where he spent a number of years as a pupil, and then he was initiated as a Brahmin of Elephant and Elora.

After a 24-year absence, Pythagoras returned to his native Samos. He was later to settle in Croton – a Greek colony in Southern Italy. Here he founded his school and laid the foundations of Pythagorean philosophy.

Pythagoras revealed the secrets of his wisdom only to a small group of his pupils. He believed that occult mathematics, music and astronomy form the triangular foundation of all arts and sciences and that their study is an essential condition for the understanding of God, nature and man. Thus, no one can be considered a pupil of Pythagoras until they master these sciences at a necessary level. This is also the message sent by the statue of Hermes, which stands in front of the University with the inscription *"Eskato Bebeloi" – "Step back, you unenlightened!"* – an order which everyone has to obey.

Pythagoras and his pupils firmly believed that everything in the world is connected in mathematics and that numbers are the supreme force which predicts and measures life in all its forms and cycles. This is a tradition which we have already encountered with Toth – Hermes Trismegistus, and the number-obsessed Mayans.

In our discussion of the Atlanteans we concluded that they interpreted the world and accumulated knowledge by means of the supreme ability of man – his intuition. Pythagoras's aim was to hone and develop this sixth sense when training his pupils.

Pythagoras' pupils, like the Mayans, revered the planet Venus, since it is the only planet which is bright enough to lighten the shadows. It can be seen immediately before Sunrise as the morning star and immediately after Sunset as the evening star. Due to these properties the ancients gave many names to Venus. They called it Vesper, the star which can be seen in the sky at sunset and another name given to Venus was the "false light", "morning star" or "Lucifer", meaning bringer of light, since it rises before the Sun. Due to its connection with the Sun, Venus has several other names: Venera, Astarta, Aphrodite, Isis and the Mother of the Gods. Pythagoras clearly acquired his precise and profound astronomical knowledge from the Egyptian oracles who understood the relationships between the heavenly bodies thousands of years before anyone else.

---

15 Zoroaster (660–583 BC) – Ancient Greek form of the name of the prophet Zaratustra. Reformer of the ancient Iranian religion. He promulgated division of light and dark as the principle of good and evil and reverence for fire.

The basic area of Pythagorean teaching is that everything in nature is divided into the three parts and to be truly wise one has to imagine every problem in the nature of a triangular diagram. According to Pythagoras:

> Concentrate upon the triangle and your problem will be two thirds resolved... Everything in nature consists of three parts.

Pythagoras thus divides the universe into three parts, which he refers to as the Supreme World, the Higher World and the Lower World. The most important of these, the Supreme World is a fine, omnipresent spiritual essence which penetrates all things and is consequently the real essence of the Supreme Deity itself, which is omnipresent, almighty and all-knowing. The Higher World is the home of the immortals and the Lower World is the home of those beings which are created by the material substance or are involved with activities linked to material substance.

The Pythagoreans did not consider 1 and 2 as numbers, since they define the two spheres of the Lower World. Pythagorean numbers begin from 3, the triangle, and 4 – the square. Added to each other, plus 1 and 2, they produce the number 10, the great number of all things, the archetype of the universe.

However, let us begin with Pythagorean numbers from 1 to 10, focusing our attention upon 3 (the triad) and 9 (the enead).

MONAD – 1: Is so called since it always remains in one and the same condition, ie., separated from the multitude. It is also referred to as the birth mind, since it is the beginning of all thoughts in the universe. Monad is the father.

DUAD – 2: Has the following symbolic names because it is always divided and represents two, not one, and they are in opposite to each other – spirit, evil, darkness, inequality, instability, movement, courage, daring, argument, material, difference and so on. Duad is the mother.

TRIAD – 3: Is the first really odd number. Monad is not considered to be a number. It is the first balance to unity. This number is called wisdom, since people organize their present, forecast their future and use the experience of the past. The number 3 challenges wisdom and understanding. Triad is the number of knowledge of music, geometry, astronomy and the science of heavenly and earthly bodies. Pythagoras taught that the cube of this number possesses the power of the lunar cycle.

The sacred role of the triad and its symbol – the triangle – originates from the fact that it consists of monad and duad. Monad is the symbol of the Holy Father, and the duad – the Great Mother. The triad, which comprises both of these, is androgynous and symbolically expresses the fact that God gives birth to all the worlds from Himself and his creative aspect is always symbolized by the triangle.

TETRAD – 4: Is considered by the Pythagoreans as the beginning which precedes every number, the root of all things, the source of nature and the most perfect of all numbers.

PENTAD – 5: Is a union of an even and odd number (2+3). The Greeks considered the pentagram as the sacred symbol of light, health and vitality.

HEXAD – 6: Is a symbol of the creation of the world, as described by the prophets and ancient Mysteries.

HEPTAD – 7: Is the sum of the number 3 (spirit, body, soul) and 4 (world) or the mystical nature of man, which consists of the triple spiritual body and four elements in material form.

OCTOAD – 8: Is sacred since it is the number of the first cube, which has eight tips and is also even – the even number closest to 10 (1- 2- 4- 8- 4- 2- 1).

ENEAD – 9: Is the first square of the odd number (3 x 3). It is connected with mistakes and insufficiencies, since it is only one number away from 10. The enead (9) is the number of man due to the nine months of embryonic development. The key words connected with 9 are ocean and horizon, since the ancients believed them to be infinite. Enead is an infinite number, since it is followed by nothing other than the infinite number 10. It is called both the border and the limit, since it includes all other numbers. Enead is the sphere of the air. It embraces the other numbers in the same way as the air embraces the Earth. Due to its resemblance to the form of sperm, 9 is also connected with the birth of life.

DECAD – 10: According to Pythagoreans it is the most supreme number, since it encompasses all arithmetic and harmonious proportions.

EIGHTEEN

Tetractys and the 47th Theorem

*I swear to he who wrote the sacred Theorem in our hearts –
an infinite and pure symbol, the primary source of our
nature and image of the gods.*
— *GOLDEN POEMS OF PYTHAGORAS*

I would like to acquaint you with the Tetractys (fig. 7 below) and the 47th theorem of Pythagoras, since they form a fundamental part of my theory.

Theon of Smirna, the philosopher and mathematician, claimed that the system of ten points, referred to as Tetractys by Pythagoras, is a particularly important symbol, since for the enlightened mind it reveals the secret of universal nature. It is interesting to note that the Pythagoreans connected it to the following oath:

> In the name of he who gave to our souls the Tetractys whose roots are in eternally living nature.

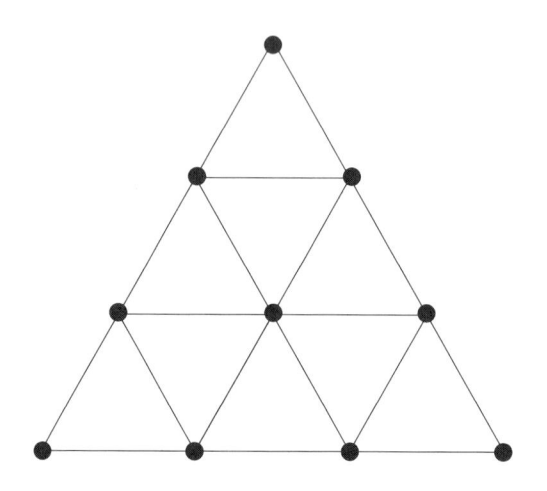

FIGURE 7

TETRACTYS AND THE 47TH THEOREM

The Pythagorean Theorem, or 47th problem of Euclid (called that because Euclid included it in a book of numbered geometry problems), is the celebrated key to philosophical mathematics. It states that:

> In the right-angled triangles the area of square on the hypotenuse is equal to the sum of the area of squares constructed from the catheti.

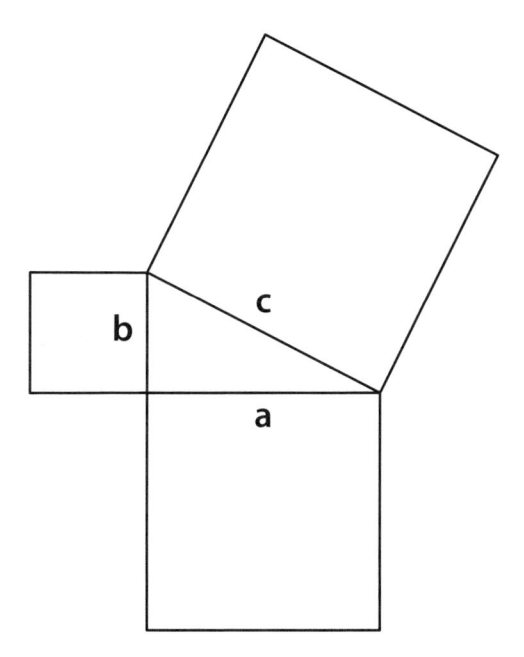

FIGURE 8
The Pythagorean Theorem

Plutarch refers to this theorem in the following way:

> Universal nature in its fullest and most complete image, according to contemporary teaching consists of three things: Reason, Matter and the results of the mutual influence which is referred to in Greek as Cosmos – a word which means both beauty and order, and the world itself. The first of these is what Plato called Idea or Father; the second is called Mother, Depository, or Birth place. The third is called Progeny or Product. There are justifiable reasons to believe that the Pythagoreans, like the Egyptians, compare universal Nature with what they refer to as "the most perfect and beautiful triangle".

According to Athanasius Kircher, the German Jesuit priest, who is compared by many with Leonardo da Vinci for his brilliance, the secret nature of the physical world is created from the most simple lines and figures. He believed that the equilateral triangle which expresses the creative work of the Holy Trinity, is the beginning of all imitations since it is the progenitor of all other multilaterals and bodies.

The next most important triangle is the isosceles triangle, symbolizing the earth and the heavenly vaults. This is followed by the right-angled triangle which contains the entire secret of the birth of nature. This triangle has one straight and two acute angles, which possess unequal sides. The right angle symbolizes the constant and unchanging action of the law of nature; the large angle means acceleration of motion, while the small angle means reduction of motion. The origin of all earthly bodies and the entire universe is contained within the right-angled triangle.

The forty-seventh theorem is an important Masonic symbol and due to its close links with the art of building is frequently referred to as the "carpenters' theorem". Many people assume that the large number of complex details on the Great Pyramid which are not understood is due to the still undiscovered applications of this theorem. The forty-seventh theorem is also the key to the relation between the three basic parts of the human being: spirit, soul and body.

NINETEEN

The Threefold Law

*The number Three reigns everywhere in the universe,
And the Monad is its beginning.*
— ZOROASTER

This law is deeply engrained in the minds of philosophers, theosophists and creators of religious movements. Pythagoras's contribution in establishing an understanding of the vital importance of the Threefold Law is extremely important. He places huge significance upon it and puts it in the heart of all sciences.

The true nature of God is depicted in the Monad, while the Duad is an expression of God's creative and reproductive capacity. The visible presence of God, or the Triad, is expressed in the following arithmetic model:

1 (Monad) + 2 (Duad) = 3 (Triad)

Further, Édouard Schuré[16] writes:

> It is the visible unfolding of God in space and time. But the real world is threefold. Man is composed of three elements, distinct yet blended into one another: body, soul and spirit. The universe likewise is divided into three concentric spheres: the natural world, the human world and the divine world. The Triad or the threefold law, therefore, is the essential law of things and the actual key to life. For this law is found at all stages of the ladder of life, from the constitution of the organic cell through the physiological constitution of the animal body, the functioning of the blood system and the cerebro-spinal system, to the hyperphysical constitution of man, universe and God. Thus, as if by enchantment it opens the internal structure of the universe to the astonished mind;

---

16 Édouard Schuré (1848-1929) – French philosopher, poet, playwright, novelist, music critic, and publicist of esoteric literature.

it reveals the infinite correspondences of macrocosm and microcosm. It acts like a light which would pass into things in order to make them transparent, and to illuminate the small and large worlds like so many magic lanterns.

Inspired by the Tetractys of Pythagoras and the words of Schuré, I reproduce these *"stages of the ladder of life"* through a system of triangles, starting from the top:

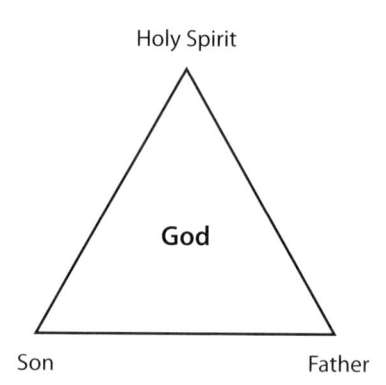

FIGURE 9 — Triangle with Holy Spirit at top, God in center, Son and Father at the base.

It is no secret that the Sun and its vital properties and principles are enshrined in the concept of the Trinity. The Triune Divinity doctrine is not just a feature of the Christian world, it is also applied in the daily lives and religions of the Hindus, Persians, Babylonians, Egyptians and Mayans.

I recently came across a valuable thought from American writer, Marie D. Jones. Marie believes that the Trinity is not just the image of God in three faces but rather a process of enlightenment – a shortcut to the Divine, which does not need a priest or a cardinal mediator in human form. This three-stage process is reflected in all of nature, science and even psychology, as a plan for the evolution of human consciousness and physical growth.

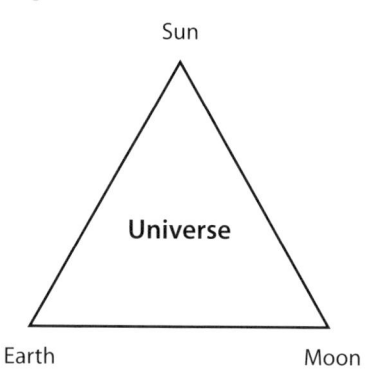

FIGURE 10 — Triangle with Sun at top, Universe in center, Earth and Moon at the base.

Where does the universe begin and end? Is it infinite? These questions concern people and scientists from many fields. Observations and studies show that the universe is expanding, which suggests that at some point in the past it had a beginning – the Big Bang.

Regardless of whether the universe is infinite or has a beginning and end, most of us accept it as what we see and feel tangibly. The foundation of Rene Descartes' philosophy lies in the notion *"I think, therefore I exist."* If we rephrase this statement with *"I see, therefore I exist"*, then this would describe the way in which many of us perceive the world.

Modern astronomers have reached the conclusion that 90% of space is composed of invisible objects and dark matter. It thus follows that only 10% of the universe is known. Despite this we have limited our understanding of the universe to just our solar system, and simplified it even to a greater extent – to the Earth, the Sun, the Moon and the billions of stars that resemble the cells of our human body. This may be because the Sun and Moon are major influences upon life on Earth and we are more concerned with those factors which impinge on our existence.

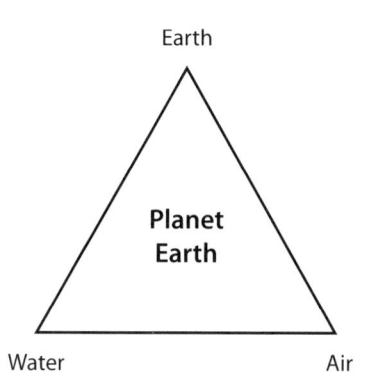

FIGURE 11: Triangle with Earth at top, Water at bottom-left, Air at bottom-right, and "Planet Earth" in the center.

Our home, the Earth was born about 16 billion years ago. However, but for almost one billion years it was hostile to any form of life. Today we use three vital elements – water, earth and air to define the nature and structure of the Earth. We and all living organisms are dependent on these elements. Water is our origin. Earth is our home. Air is our life. Life originated in water and it is no surprise that two thirds of our body is made up of water. The effect of the oceans and seas on all of us is obvious. Tides happen within our own bodies because we carry within ourselves particles of the world ocean.

Around 350 million years ago, life left the oceans and came out onto dry land. The earth satisfies our physiological needs by providing essential nutrients. By consuming food we enable our bodies to recreate while discarding dead cells back into the soil. In this sense human beings are constantly transformed by recycling the earth.

Air is connected to the most important physiological process – breathing. The rhythmic inhalation and exhalation of oxygen and carbon dioxide determines the rhythm of our existence. The interaction between air and every single living being is the most convincing evidence of the importance of rhythm for life on our planet.

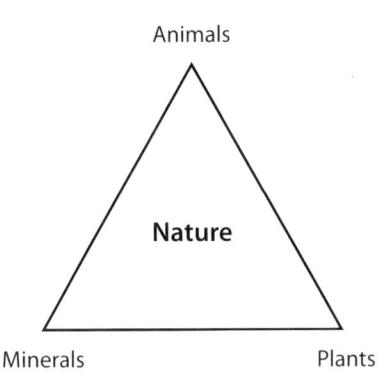

FIGURE 12

The world of minerals, plants and animals (including humans) is the Trinity which forms the harmonic pulse of Nature. In Nature we find the footprints of time and the breath of God. The natural balance observed in Nature can save lives and cure diseases by eliminating pollution and decay. Thus even today we see confirmation of the ancient axioms:

Nature contains Nature.

Nature rejoices in her own nature.

Nature surmounts Nature.

Nature cannot be amended but in her own nature.

```
         Mind & Soul
             /\
            /  \
           /    \
          / Human\
         /        \
        /_____\
     Body            Spirit
```

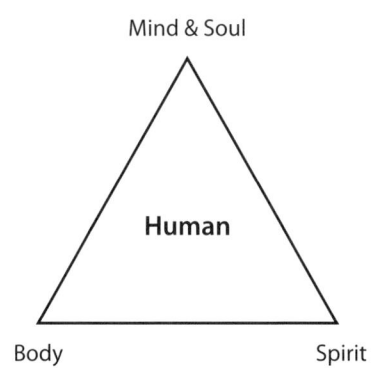

FIGURE 13

The evolution of humankind gives us the following sequence: body, spirit, mind and soul. Today we believe that evolved modern humans bear the mark of high intelligence and understanding. Is this really so? Millions of years ago humans discarded their tails and equipped themselves with a new weapon vital for survival – the mind.

The mind develops along with the expansion of consciousness and spirit. The five primary senses, sight, hearing, smell, taste and touch, send information to the brain about the world around us. This information is translated into electromagnetic waves which reach the brain and are then interpreted by our mind. However, what if the world around us is not as our mind sees it? According to quantum physics, we and the world around us are nothing but electromagnetic waves vibrating at different frequencies, living in an infinite and uniform informational field.

```
         Neocortex
             /\
            /  \
           /    \
          / Brain\
         /        \
        /_____\
  Ancient Brain    Limbic System
```

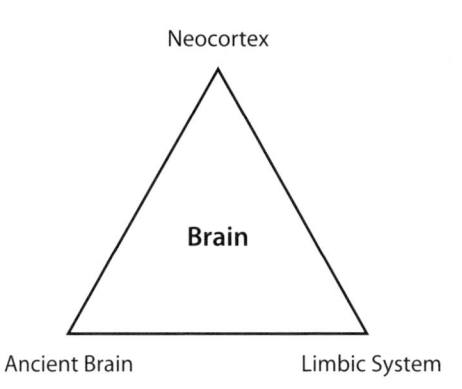

FIGURE 14

The human brain in essence is Triune; three structures, each of which has evolved in a different time period. The first structure is the ancient brain which helps us to survive and is similar to the brain of reptiles. The second developed later and has a more sophisticated limbic system. The third structure, the neocortex is the most recent. The lack of integration between the three brains today is described by neurologist Paul D. MacLean in the term '*Schizophysiologia*'.

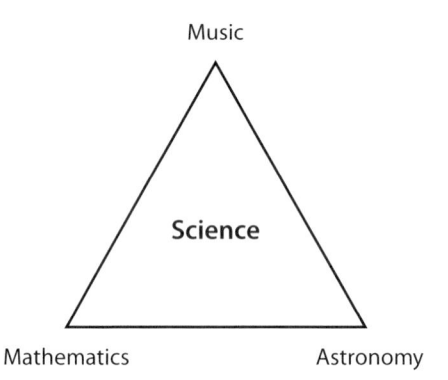

FIGURE 15

According to wise Pythagoras as we saw earlier, the triangular foundation of all sciences and arts lies in mathematics, music and astronomy. Learning and mastering the trinity is an essential part of understanding God, Man and Nature. According to Hermes Trismegistus:

> And yet though this is so, there are in all the beings senses, in that they cannot without senses be. But Gnosis is far different from sense. For sense is brought about by that which hath the mastery o'er us, while Gnosis is the end of science, and science is God's gift. All science is incorporeal, the instrument it uses being the mind, just as the mind employs the body. Both then come into bodies, (I mean) both things that are cognizable by mind alone and things material. For all things must consist out of antithesis and contrariety; and this can otherwise not be.

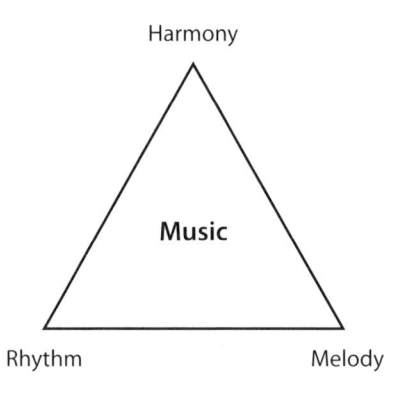

FIGURE 16

Since rhythm is the main topic of this book and since it is the basic building block in Music, the next trinity I would like to present is Rhythm, Melody and Harmony. Long before we were able to think rationally and communicate verbally, human beings communicated and expressed their feelings and emotions through the language of percussion instruments – stones, bones, wood, drums, rattles and metals.

These instruments were the tools which maintained humanity's direct connection with the natural sounds and rhythms of their environment. Melody occurs with the first songs in praise of God and is mostly associated with church services. Gregorian chants are an eloquent example of this. Rhythm and melody developed between 500-600 AD., reaching more complex models of performance and perception.

In around 1450 AD., the foundations and rules of tonal harmony were determined at a convention of clergy and composers. The main objective was to establish a common sound and style avoiding unpleasant sound or dissonance. Certain melodic and harmonic progressions and intervals were forbidden and many musicians and composers who broke the rules were declared heretics and condemned to burn at the stake.

Harmony is to music what evolution is to the mind. The established dogmas and models define what is good and what is bad in music, or what is allowed and what is not. In other words the composer's emotions, feelings and thoughts are channelled in a destined direction. *We are all composers, regardless of whether we create music or create our own lives.* The musical elements of rhythm, melody and harmony dictate the quality of our daily lives. The secret of creating a valuable composition lies in finding the right balance between these three elements.

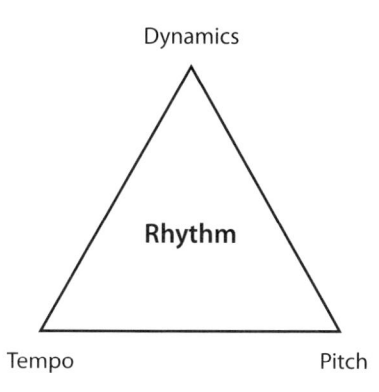

FIGURE 17

Once again we return to rhythm. This time we will go into a more detailed definition of Rhythm which differs from the previously discussed factors of Time, Space and Motion. Later in this book we will be able to look at this Trinity in detail and see how Tempo, Dynamics and Pitch are determined by Time, Space and Motion.

TWENTY

Microcosm and Macrocosm

As above, so below; as below, so above.
— THE KYBALION

According to this great Hermetic Principle there is a close correspondence between all levels of manifestation, life and being. The same laws and principles are applicable to all of us and everything around us. They find expression on every level through our unique nature. Understanding this principle allows us to explain many phenomena in nature and in life which are beyond the horizon of our perception and capabilities. The ancient Hermetic thought, *"as above, so below; as below, so above"*, is a universal law which enables us to peer into the world of the unknown.

In the previous chapter we saw different types of Trinities which formed a micro-macrocosm principle. I want now to look at *"The Principle of Correspondence"* in which we choose and compare the three Trinities, at the top, middle and bottom of the scale.

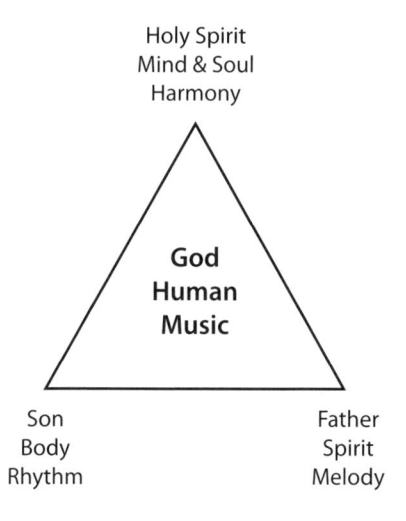

```
              Holy Spirit
              Mind & Soul
               Harmony
                  △
                 /  \
                /    \
               / God  \
              / Human  \
             /  Music   \
            /_____\
        Son                Father
        Body               Spirit
        Rhythm             Melody
```

FIGURE 18

79

God or Human is the Trinity of the Son - materialised in the Body; the Father - the Spirit and Knowledge; the Holy Spirit - the highest Mind. Music as man's work is a mirror which we can look into and see our development. As a result of these interrelations, and often captivated by magical sounds, we are witnesses of God's presence in music.

This analysis of three-fold nature can be applied to everything which surrounds us. As another example there is the Universal Trinity – the Earth, Moon and Sun. If we use only the Sun, we get the following Trinity:

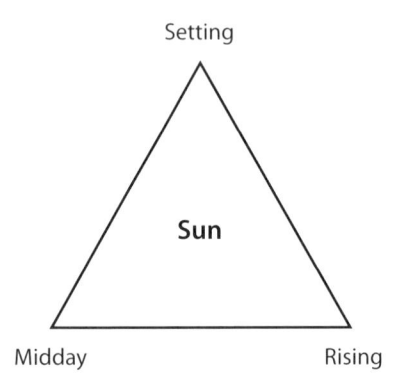

```
              Setting
                 △
                ╱ ╲
               ╱   ╲
              ╱ Sun ╲
             ╱       ╲
            ╱_____╲
        Midday        Rising
```

FIGURE 19

The distinguished esoteric American author Manly Palmer Hall wrote:

> The origin of the Trinity is obvious to anyone who will observe the daily manifestations of the sun. This orb, being the symbol of all Light, has three distinct phases: rising, midday, and setting. The philosophers therefore divided the life of all things into three distinct parts: growth, maturity, and decay. Between the twilight of dawn and the twilight of evening is the high noon of resplendent glory. God the Father, the Creator of the world, is symbolized by the dawn. His colour is blue, because the sun rising in the morning is veiled in blue mist. God the Son, the Illuminating One sent to bear witness of His Father before all the worlds, is the celestial globe at noonday, radiant and magnificent, the maned Lion of Judah, the Golden-haired Saviour of the World. Yellow is His colour and His power is without end. God the Holy Ghost is the sunset phase, when the orb of day, robed in flaming red, rests for a moment upon the horizon line and then vanishes into the darkness of the night to wander the lower worlds and later rise again triumphant from the embrace of darkness.

If you are willing to try a challenge, look for Trinities and correspondences at the different levels of the scale given in the last chapter.

TWENTY-ONE

Rhythm and Tetractys

*Man is a microcosm, or a little world, because he is an extract
from all the stars and planets of the whole firmament,
from the earth and the elements; and so he is their quintessence.*
— PARACELSUS [17]

Now let us look at rhythm, since it is an essential part of this book. We began with the triangular door of Pakal's tomb and the Hermetic Philosophy of the Fundamental Truth located behind Time, Space and Motion. We made a journey in search of the key to this truth. Our journey was circular and we are now facing the same door with more knowledge and opportunities. Now is the time to add the missing factor to our chart, which is the definition of rhythm – the circle that symbolizes the cycles:

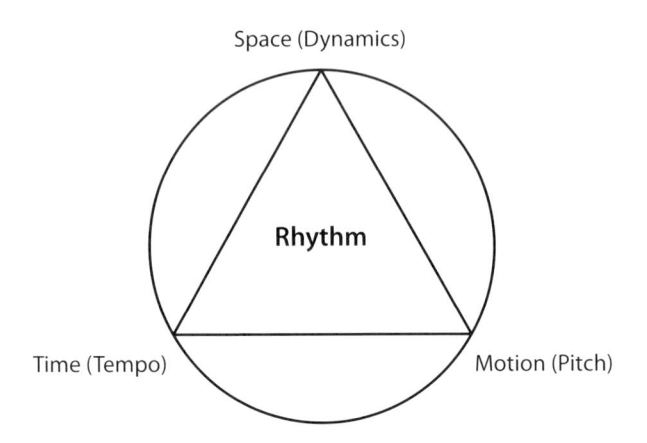

FIGURE 20

---

17 Philippus Aureolus Theophrastus Bombastus von Hohenheim, known as Paracelsus (1493 – 1541) – Swiss doctor, academic, alchemist, astrologer and philosopher.

RHYTHM AND TETRACTYS

Between the brackets you will see the reduced model of rhythm which we discussed in the previous chapters. The three factors, Tempo, Dynamics and Pitch, lead us to a more detailed definition and understanding of rhythm. They are concepts and terms which contain a musical nuance but also have a direct relation and application in every breath of the cosmos, nature and ourselves. Furthermore, everything depends on them.

They correspond to already established elements in the following way: Tempo is determined by Time and its speed; Dynamics is defined by the Space required for the performance of specific amplitude which sets up the power; and Pitch is identified by the Motions of the vibrations.

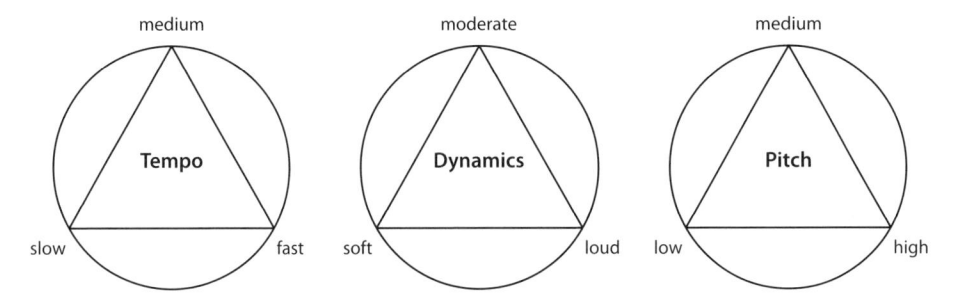

FIGURE 21

At this point we will stop the reduction which we started from the Trinity of God, and we will return to the Tetractys – the symbol of universal and eternal nature. If we connect the ten points of the Tetractys, we will obtain nine triangles in which we can insert the cells which form the last three Trinities:

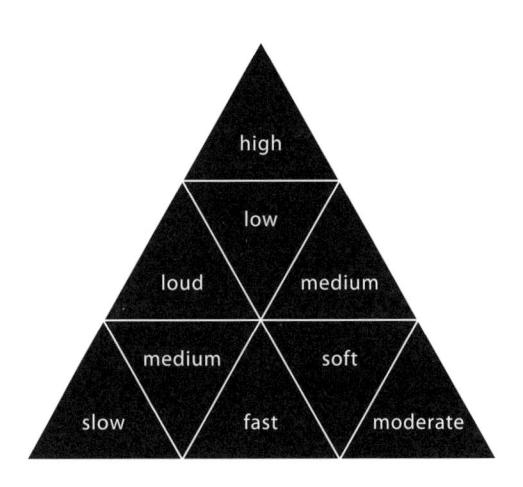

FIGURE 22

If we produce all possible permutations[18] of these 9 elements, we will obtain 27 models:

> slow (tempo) - soft (dynamics) - low (pitch)
>
> slow (tempo) - moderate (dynamics) - medium (pitch)
>
> slow (tempo) - loud (dynamics) - high (pitch), etc.

These 27 rhythmic patterns are represented by the 27 peaks shaped by the nine triangles in the Tetractys. Let us now summarize and bring together all that information in a single diagram:

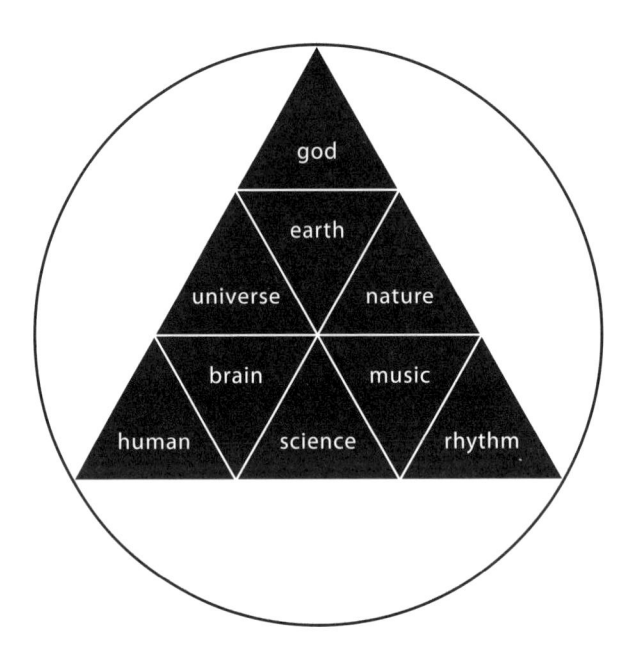

FIGURE 23

The circle symbolizes Unity and the Cycle. Its three components (centre, radius and circle) represent the Divine Trinity. The large triangle in this diagram representing The All is filled by nine Trinities (triangles) of the micro-macrocosmic scale.

---

18 Permutation – Every arrangement of given elements is called a permutation (permutation without repetition) of these elements. In a given permutation of elements each element participates only once and its place in the permutation is essential.

The 27 models which characterize the various forms of vibration/rhythm are represented by the 27 peaks. They are the particles which with their cyclical oscillation bring life to the nine Trinities and to the big triangle itself. The Tempo, Pitch and Dynamics with which they vibrate determine the spectrum of their manifestation and existence.

According to the Kabbalah [19] the three unused corner points of the Tetractys are the triple invisible cause of the universe.

In this diagram we can see the manifestation of each of the Seven Hermetic Principles. It allows us to understand the meaning of the expression *"from outside is like inside; the small is like the big."* According to Hermes Trismegistus, this is one of the primary keys to knowledge. The Sufi of the 12th century summed it up in the direct phrase *"microcosm is the macrocosm"*, while the Hindu Vishvasara tantra states that, *"Whatever is here, is everywhere"*. Here, side by side, the wisdom of the Ancients pulsates with the contemporary concepts of quantum physics regarding the holographic nature of the universe to be found in the smallest particle, and vice versa.

---

19 Kabbalah – mystical teaching and traditions whose basic idea is that every person in connected with God and that we need to work on the different aspects of our soul in order to attain harmony.

TWENTY-TWO

13

> *The moral test was a more serious one. Suddenly, without the least preparation, the would-be disciple would one fine morning find himself imprisoned in an empty, dismal-looking cell. A slate was given him and he was coldly ordered to discover the meaning of one of the Pythagorean symbols, as, for instance: What is the signification of the triangle inscribed in a circle?*
> — ÉDOUARD SCHURÉ

If we continue our analysis of the diagram (fig. 23 in the previous chapter) and imagine it as numbers, the following will be obtained:

1 3 9 27

Circle – 1 (Many people would associate the circle with zero but Pythagoras teaches us that the symbol of the point is the number 1. If we increase the size of the point it will become a circle.)

Large triangle – 3

Nine small triangles – 9

The apexes of the small triangles – 27

The first two geometrical figures and numbers produce 13 – a number to which special attention will be paid in this chapter (fig. 24).

The Mayans believed the number 1 to symbolize Unity, while 3 was for them the number of Rhythm. If we unite the two designates in the number 13, we will obtain the Unified Rhythm, or a matrix within each particle of the universe combines mutually and exists.

Is it coincidental that 3113 BC., the year when the "birth of Venus" marked

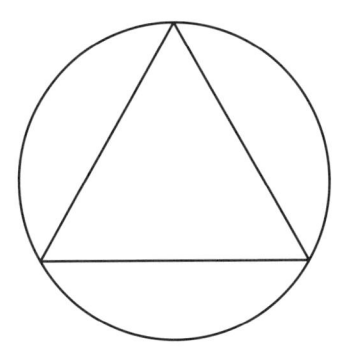

FIGURE 24

the beginning of their calendar and the "Long Count", consists of two "thirteens" (31 – anagram and 13)? This is a question to which no one can give a categorical answer, but we can doubtlessly look into the life, culture and beliefs of the Mayans to discover what the number 13 meant for them.

Although the number 13 in our days is associated with fatalism, bad luck and unhappiness, for the ancient civilizations it was a sacred number. This is true not only for the Mexican cultures of the Mayans and Aztecs but many other world religions. In the Christian religion, for example, the number 13 plays an exceptionally important role: Jesus and his twelve Apostles made up a group of 13. The Zodiac consists of 12 signs but in its entirety - 13. "Genesis" describes God creating the world in 7 days and 6 nights, which is symbolically represented by means of the Judaic Menorah.

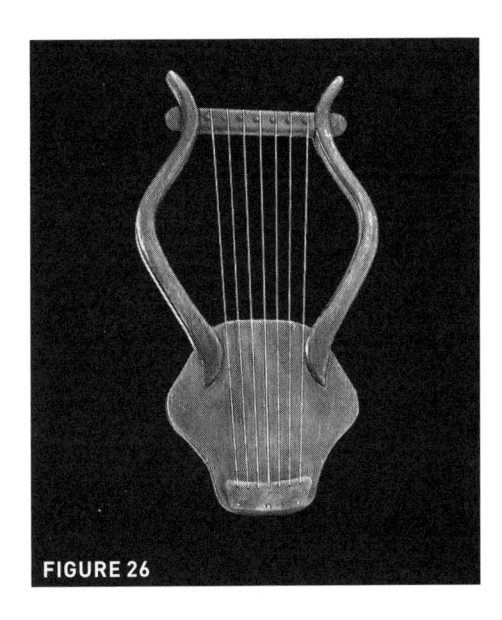

FIGURE 25

FIGURE 26

The number 13 can be seen in fig. 25 not only in the product of the seven burning lamps (days) and the six empty spaces (nights), but also as a simple configuration of shapes – one straight lamp stalk and three curved double lamp stalks.

Identical symbolism and logic can be seen in Orpheus' lyre (fig. 26), in which the seven strings and their resonance symbolize the days, while the six spaces and corresponding silences represent the nights.

For the Mayans and the other Central American civilizations, the process of creation was connected with the thirteen heavenly kingdoms, each one of which corresponds to specific evolutionary processes and the dominant divinity:

Heavenly kingdom	Divinity	Stage of growth
1.	Xiuhtecuhtli: God of Fire and Time	Sowing
2.	Tlaltecuhtli: God of the Earth	
3.	Chalchiuhtlicue: Goddess of Water	Germination
4.	Tonatiuh: God of the Sun and Warriors	
5.	Tlacoteotl: Goddess of Love and Childbirth	Sprouting
6.	Mictlantecuhtli: God of Death	
7.	Cinteotl: God of Maize and Sustenance	Proliferation
8.	Tlaloc: God of Rain and War	
9.	Quetzalcoatl: God of Light	Budding
10.	Tezcatlipoca: God of Darkness	
11.	Yohualticitl: Goddess of Birth	Flowering
12.	Tlahuizcalpantecuhtli: God before Dawn	
13.	Ometeotl/Omecinatl: Dual-Creator God	Fruition

FIGURE 27

The odd numbers are all connected with the divine light and day and the even numbers are connected with dark and the night. The conclusion which we can draw from this is that the seven odd and six even-numbered heavens are not different from the seven days and nights of Divine Creation.

Everything which we have discussed until this moment has been sealed with brilliant precision by the Mayan architects within the pyramids of Kukulkan at Chichen Itza. (See fig. 28) When the nine-storied pyramid is looked at from a particular angle only possible during the spring and autumn solstice, then 13 triangles can be seen formed by the falling light – 7 white (days) and 6 dark (nights). Apart from the fact that the triangles symbolise the thirteen heavens, they also represent the body of the snake descending to earth while its head is at the base of the pyramid. This is the Feathered Snake (Quetzalcoatl) and its descent to earth.

FIGURE 28

Note that apart from the number 13, the pyramid also reveals the symbols and numbers which we have talked about until now:

1   appears in the cyclical repetition of the spring and autumn solstice without which the process remains invisible.

3   appears in all triangles which we observe, or if we make the simple calculation:

$$13 \times 3 \text{ (peaks of the triangle)} = 39$$
$$3 + 9 = 12$$
$$1 + 2 = 3$$

9   nine stories of the pyramid.
27 is also 9, or 2 + 7 = 9

This pyramid also contains encoded information which reveals more than ordinary numbers. It is something which brings us back to the dawn of our existence and forms a bridge to the unknown future in a measured and Unified Rhythm (13). It confirms the enormous wisdom and knowledge of the ancients who left messages in the hope that they will one day be decoded and used correctly by contemporary man.

TWENTY-THREE

The Evolution of Consciousness

To be co-creators, we need to know what the canvas we are to work on looks like and what its format is. If we choose to surf on the cosmic plan, we had better know what the rhythm of divine process is.
— CARL JOHAN CALLEMAN

Dr. Carl Johan Calleman, the Swedish academic, is one of the people who have dedicated their lives to the study of ancient mysteries and messages left by the Mayans. In his works he not only studies in great detail their secrets, but also gives a very well argumented and full explanation of the evolutionary process of consciousness.

He believes that evolution and consciousness move in a strictly determined and delineated rhythm and that all this was understood and expressed by the Mayans. In addition to their architectural monuments, the main source for these claims is to be found in their calendar. Due to the large volume of information contained in the Mayan calendar, we will not go into this theme in detail here, but we shall look at the basic concepts connected with the Mayan concept of chronicling time.

Let us, therefore, return to the Kukulkan pyramid and its 9 stories symbolising the 9 underworlds. In Mesoamerican mythology, in addition to the 13 heavenly kingdoms, there are also 9 underworlds. Although it is impossible to attain a complete understanding of these underworlds, we can assume that they are nine successively activated structures of consciousness linked to the internal core of the earth. This theory is confirmed by the stela found in Coba, Jukatan and the decoded symbols inscribed upon it.

This 1,300 year-old funereal stone bears inscriptions which not only describe with accuracy the date on which the "Great Counting" (3113 BC.,) begins, but also those nine periods of the evolution of consciousness.

FIGURE 29

Dr. Calleman manages to systematize this information in the following table:

Underworld	Duration	Level of consciousness (events)	Level of evolution
Universal	13 uinals (260 days)	Evolution of Cosmic consciousness (revolution of consciousness)	Ninth
Galactic	13 tuns (12.8 years)	Evolution of Galactic consciousness (internet/global economy)	Eighth
Planetary	13 katuns (256 years)	Evolution of Global consciousness (industrial age)	Seventh
National	13 baktuns (5.125 years)	Evolution of Civilized consciousness (written language)	Sixth
Regional	13 piktuns (102,000 years)	Evolution of Human consciousness (spoken language)	Fifth
Tribal	13 kalabtuns (2 million years)	Evolution of Hominid consciousness (first humans)	Fourth
Familial	13 kinchiltuns (41 million years)	Evolution of Anthropoid consciousness (first primates)	Third
Mammalian	13 alautuns (820 million years)	Evolution of Mammalian consciousness (first animals)	Second
Cellular	13 hablatuns (16.4 billion years)	Evolution of Cellular consciousness (Big Bang)	First

FIGURE 30

Clearly Dr. Calleman named every single period in the evolution of the consciousness (underworlds). Then he made the necessary calculations to establish that these stages correspond to scientific and historical dates. These dates were defined only about 50 years ago. For example, the cycles which he describes relate to the evolutionary process which began 16.4 billion years ago.

Cosmologists claim that the universe was created about 15 billion years ago which is close enough to the date given by the Mayans – 13 hablatuns or 13×20^7 tuns (1 tun is equal to 360 days). The other dates shown on the stela are either the same as those described in scientific theories to be important evolutionary transitions or sufficiently close to them.

Only 150 years ago geologists and biologists began to realize that humankind was born in the very distant past. Charles Darwin published his work, *The Origin of the Species* in 1859, but the work was noted only at the middle of the 20th century, thanks to the work of Mary and Louis Leakey. The dates on the stela were decoded in about 1950, which makes the synchronization between these two events quite unique.

It is particularly interesting that each subsequent period is shorter than the previous and that there is a twenty-fold increase in acceleration which generates a specific rhythm, reminiscent of the pyramid. The time which it takes for the changes to occur to consciousness at each stage, is shorter and the speed is constantly increasing. Barbara Hand Clow, the internationally acclaimed ceremonial teacher and author, makes the following comment regarding Dr. Calleman's model:

> Previous creations became part of later creations, and this evolution is generated by cycles that are twenty times shorter than the previous Underworld. Since each cycle is twenty times shorter than the previous one, time is accelerating by a factor of twenty during the opening of each Underworld.

Perhaps you realize that we are looking at the cross section of the Kukulkan with its nine stories (underworlds) and thirteen triangles (heavenly kingdoms – 7 days and 6 nights). The Mayans immortalized this divine composition in a grandiose

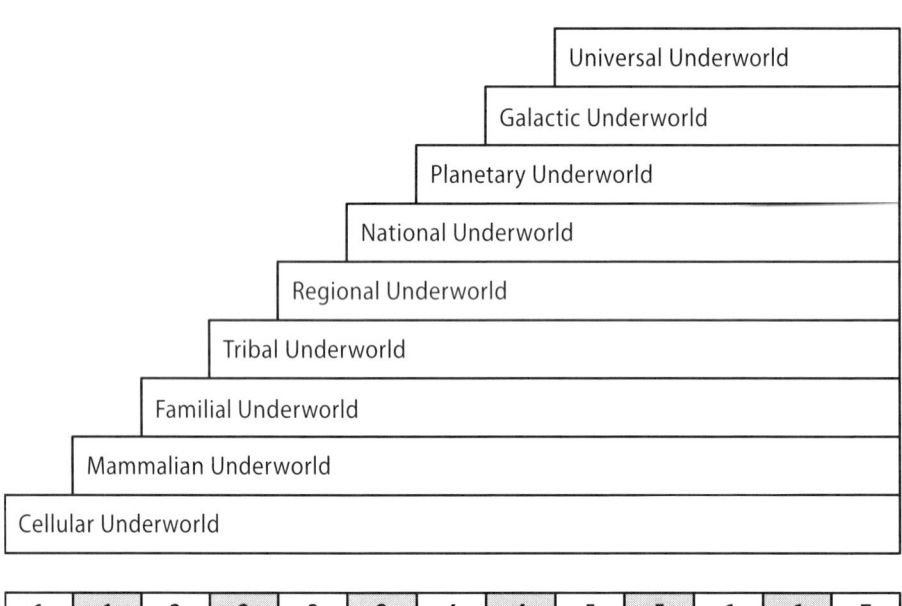

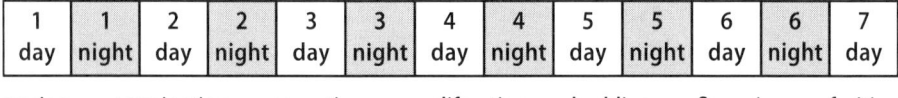

FIGURE 31

monument, reflecting the thirteen stages in the development of each cycle and the entire evolutionary process. These stages are characterized by periods of creation of a new level (through the days) and the integration and confirmation of the new (through the nights).

As we can see, the process of creation (sowing, germination, sprouting, proliferation, budding, flowering, fruition) is inscribed with total accuracy in the overall creative concept. The Mayans discovered the evolutionary model in the same way as it is known to modern science – 9 periods in which the transformation of consciousness and evolutionary changes take place with a Unified Rhythm (13).

It is a unified rhythm in which the tempo gradually becomes faster, the dynamic stronger and the pitch higher.

What would this rhythm look like?

TWENTY-FOUR

Rhythm and Polyrhythm

*All these rhythms are in harmony with each other.
There are rhythms within rhythms within rhythms.
And these drumbeats echo all around us and within us.
We are not outsiders to the process; we are part of it,
throbbing to the pulse of the universe.*

— DEEPAK CHOPRA

Close your eyes slowly. Take a deep breath and exhale. Continue breathing while trying to visualize and hear the rhythm, gradually becoming faster, stronger and higher. Imagine it as a movement, direction and amplitude. Draw graphics in your mind. Follow the line upwards to a point of climax. As you inhale again, imagine the movement of air slowly entering your body drawing the same line upwards. The outside world enters you. Hold this breath for a moment as you get to the top of the line, the point of climax, and your inner and outer worlds join together. Now exhale slowly while following the descent line – your inner world flows to the outside one.

In this process you inhale the *"scent"* of the world and bring it into your system. When you exhale, you send your inner world to the outer world. The moment between inhaling and exhaling is the climax point: SILENCE – the balance between your world and outside world. The graphic which describes the rhythm of *the* most important process for us (breathing in - breathing out) forms the shape of an arch:

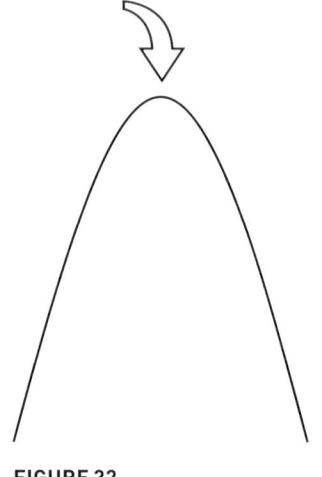

FIGURE 32

Another triangle which represents the Trinity of breath:

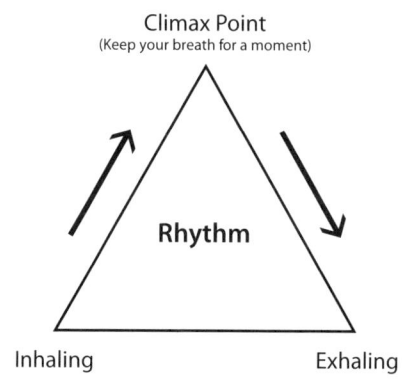

FIGURE 33

This process of contraction and relaxation, tension and release is fundamental to the whole universe. Days and nights, tides, lunar cycles, seasons, migration of birds and animals, and plant growth, all pulse with this rhythm but in different frequencies.

In the Kukulkan pyramid in Chichen Itza this same rhythm plays a particularly important role. This can be seen at the micro - macrocosmic level. As we saw in the last chapter, the seven days and six nights form a developmental pattern which describes steps and stages with their specific climaxes. These stages include sowing, germination, sprouting, proliferation, budding and flowering. They all lead to the final climactic fruition on the seventh day.

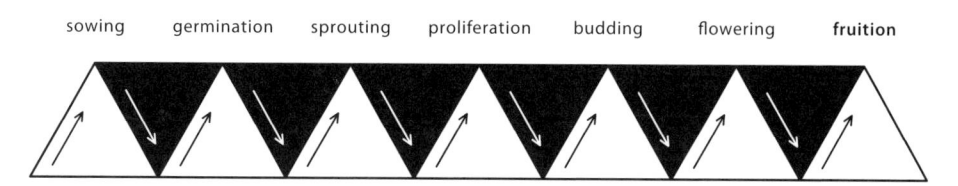

FIGURE 34

This rhythm is characteristic for each of the nine Underground Worlds and is associated with the evolution of consciousness. Each of them is different from previous with faster tempo, louder dynamics and higher pitch. With their variety of days and nights and climax points, all these rhythms create an endless polyrhythmic symphony leading to the greatest climax.

What is Polyrhythm? It is the simultaneous sounding of two or more independent rhythms. The use of this term is specific to music, especially those styles which emphasize the diversity of rhythmic patterns played by various percussion instruments. These rhythms usually follow certain patterns which repeat or end depending on the personal taste and decision of the composer and performer. Although we find musical polyrhythm examples in all ethnic groups, African folk music, in particular from Western Africa, is known for the richest polyrhythmic percussion music.

In the African tribal ensemble the voices of drums speak with a variety of pitches and timbres. The specific rhythm lines are like intertwined jungle vines which embrace a pre-established fundamental pulse. This pulse reflects the earth's pulse and the heartbeat of each member of the tribe. Although each performer has a certain and individual rhythmic role, the cascade of sounds and rhythms, colours and forms, gestures and movements creates an impressive synchronistic *"picture"* entitled *"Polyrhythm"*.

When I hear that word, I immediately imagine a huge, beautiful bouquet. Each flower in this bouquet, is arranged in such a way that its fragrance blends with the others' in an aromatic nectar. Its colours blend with the colours of the other flowers and form a colourful tapestry. Then I begin to hear the sounds and their voices singing a song – each flower is part of the bouquet and the bouquet is part of every single flower. They even begin to sway to the beat of their natural, elegant dance and each flower follows its own distinct step.

If we remove one of them, the bouquet will no longer be the same. As you see, the term Polyrhythm can be used not only in music. We are Polyrhythm. The universe is Polyrhythm. Everything around us is vibration – a sequence of motion and rest, sound and silence which by itself is a rhythm.

PART III

Alchemy

TWENTY-FIVE

The Capstone

As a rough and unfinished block, man is taken from the quarry and by the secret culture of the Mysteries gradually transformed into a true and perfect pyramidal capstone. The temple is complete only when the initiate himself becomes the living apex through which the divine power is focused into the diverging structure below.
— MANLY PALMER HALL

As we begin Part Three, I would like to summarize the ideas up to this point: One of the key questions we asked ourselves was connected to the formulae by which we control our mental vibrations. According to Hermetic knowledge, the understanding of "*The Principle of Vibration*", and its application with appropriate formulae, can allow us to reach that level. However, these formulae are not apparent in the ancient texts. So we embarked on an adventure to find the door and the key to this hidden knowledge.

The fundamental purpose of our search is vibration – the most important element in the creation of the world of minerals, plants, animals and humans. Each form of existence is created by a gradual transformation of vibration. They differ in length, width, colour, impact, sound and rhythm. We have established equality between vibration – rhythm - time and have determined their triune nature as the foundation of the micro-macrocosmic scale of manifestation.

We have discussed the architectural phenomena and philosophies encoded in the symbols of ancient wisdom. We have uncovered many interesting facts and thoughts and have drawn the conclusions required to continue our journey.

Now we need to go deeper into our human nature to get to the essence of the main objective. Have you ever considered how precisely we can calculate the Sun's diameter, determine the distance from the Earth to the Moon, find new species and study their molecular structure, but when it comes to discovering oneself we have difficulties?

We know so much about the surrounding world, but when someone asks us what the soul is and how our thoughts are created, we simply shrug our shoulders. Perhaps this ignorance reveals the problem that we are looking for happiness not in ourselves, but in the objects which surround us.

Zen Buddhists believe that in order to find Buddha in our own nature, to know the truth and hence happiness, we do not need to study the world around us. In order to achieve marginal reality, we need only to look inside ourselves and allow our higher self to mature. The essential feature of Hindu philosophy is the principle of studying one's inner world. Socrates believed that one cannot achieve happiness; not because we do not want it but because we do not know what it consists of. The great Pythagoras wrote about inner happiness in his legendary Golden verses:

You shall likewise know that according to Law,
the nature of this universe is in all things alike,

So that you shall not hope for what you ought not to hope;
and nothing in this world shall be hidden from you.

You will likewise know that human beings bring on their
own misfortunes, voluntarily and of their own free choice.

Unhappy that they are! They neither see nor understand
that what is best for them is within them.

Few know how to deliver themselves out of their misfortunes.

Such is the fate that blinds humanity, and takes away their senses.

Like huge barrels they roll to and fro, always oppressed
with innumerable problems.

For fatal strife, seemingly innate, pursues them everywhere,
tossing them up and down; nor do they perceive this.

Instead of provoking and stirring up strife, they ought,
by yielding, to avoid it.

The process of searching for and finding happiness is a basic human desire. It defines the meaning of our existence. We all want it, one way or another. Some of us truly succeed, while others wander through the labyrinth of life. Happiness is harmony – just the right combination of rhythm, melody and silence. Nobody wants to be in the circle of pain, fear and anxiety; the main expressions of disharmony. We are all to one extent or another seeking for harmony, in whatever physical or spiritual expression.

The constant search for harmony (happiness) is encoded in human nature but very often we do not choose the right path. The ancient sages wrote about the path which leads deep inside us. Our modern civilization has unfortunately lost its way in the midst of time. Lost – like the capstone – the stone that crowned the very top of the Great Pyramid at Giza. The capstone is a miniature replica of the entire structure of the pyramid. In this way the pyramid can be defined as the universe and the capstone as man. Continuing this sequence of analogies, the mind is the capstone of Man, the spirit is the capstone of mind, and God as a prototype of the entire structure is the capstone of spirit.

This was discussed in Part Two; the triangles represented the pyramid and its capstone in a two-dimensional plan. We see therefore that the path leads to our inner self and we must find our lost capstone in order to achieve the desired harmony.

In fact we ourselves are pyramids. The triangular shape expresses our posture during the meditative exercises which lead us into a deeper relationship with ourselves. The three main chambers of the Great Pyramid of Giza correspond to the heart, brain and reproductive system – the spiritual centres of the human physical structure.

In 1859, the British publisher and author, John Taylor, wrote, *The Great Pyramid; Why was it Built & Who Built It?* For the first time, Taylor presented the theory that the Egyptians had incorporated the number π into the construction of this unique monument, showing that π was known to them long before the presumed date of its discovery. Assuming that the capstone had once stood in place, Taylor calculated that the height of the Great Pyramid was 148.1328 m (486 feet). If we reduce this number using the Pythagorean approach, we obtain the following:

$$1 + 4 + 8 + 1 + 3 + 2 + 8 = 27 = 2 + 7 = 9$$

or

$$4 + 8 + 6 = 18 = 1 + 8 = 9$$

Here, we must recall another number – the great harmonic number of Maya – 1,366 560, and its simplification process:

$$1 + 3 + 6 + 6 + 5 + 6 + 0 = 27 = 2 + 7 = 9$$

Coincidence!? Again!? I would say that this is yet another confirmation of the synchronization of the global truth. Once again we obtain the number 9 which is not only the sacred number of Mayans, but Man's symbol as well. The number of Man corresponds to the pyramid's height and reinforces the idea of the human being exemplified in architecture. It is important to remember that the capstone is the final piece which completes this number!

Where is this triangular stone which gives integrity and completeness to the whole structure? It may be the same "*stone*" sought after by the ancient alchemists – the so-called "*Philosopher's Stone*". Does the triangular capstone represent the ancient Hermetic formulae? The formulae which we are looking for!

TWENTY-SIX

Alchemy and the Philosopher's Stone

The alchemist imitates nature and by his actions recreates and accelerates its processes. Thanks to the principle of the analogy which directs alchemy, it may influence both nature and man. It reflects divine creation and action.
— JEAN-PAUL CORSETTI[20]

Very frequently when we use the word "alchemist" we imagine the image of a charlatan who has dedicated his life to the pointless cause of trying to turn base metal into gold.

It could be said that there is a certain amount of truth in this association, but we must not think of serious alchemists as mad old men poring over beakers filled with a boiling coloured liquid. This idea is clearly incomplete and groundless. No one knows where the world "alchemy" comes from. The best explanation is that it means the "art of the country of the Khem".

The cradle of this ancient knowledge is Egypt, or Khem, as it is known by the Arabs. From here the details of this mystical science were passed on to the West. There is a centuries-old legend about the secrets of alchemy that they originate from the Egyptian teachings of Toth – Hermes Trismegistus and the secret haldeic teaching disseminated by Zarathustra. The first alchemist essays, such as that by Zosim the Greek alchemist, were profoundly influenced by Hermeticism and date from the 3rd century.

Like every valuable art and science, alchemy was patronized by the gods. The nuances and secrets of alchemy were revealed by them only to select humans. The creators and guardians of these ancient formulae were considered to be Thoth – Hermes Trismegistus, Osiris, Isis and kings and queens such as Cheops and Cleopatra.

---

20 Jean-Paul Corsetti (1956) – Essayist, critic and one of the most famous researchers into the esotericism in France.

The list of celebrated alchemists also includes the names of some of the greatest thinkers and academics of their times such as Jabir, Al Razi, Albert the Great, Saint Thomas Aquinas, Robert Bacon, Helvetius and others. It is important to note that when alchemy reached its apogee, there was no definite boundary between science and magic. In our days we experience huge difficulty when we have to believe that the stars, planets, shapes and numbers can affect and influence human life. We are even inclined to consider it as superstition, while the people of that time who created the foundations of modern science, accepted it as something completely normal.

Gold has been considered the most precious metal even from the most ancient of times. Long before the appearance of alchemy, it was considered the most perfect metal and acquired symbolic meanings comparing it with light, wisdom, nobility and perfection. Most people believe that the main purpose of alchemy was to turn base metals into gold, but they omit its most important mission – to create the conditions for the soul to transcend its normal state and achieve perfection.

The Philosopher's Stone is a cherished aim to which many people have devoted their lives. They spend centuries stubbornly searching for that mystical object which is actually not a stone but a substance. It is a substance which they believed they could attain with divine help and by subjecting specific raw materials to complex and long-lasting processes.

In their search for the Philosopher's Stone, alchemists used an amazing variety of substances. Copper and lead, sulphur and arsenic, urine and gall are only a small part of them. The substances were mixed and divided, heated and cooled, transformed into steam and solids, and sometimes just left to rot.

As we can see the hard work and efforts of the alchemists in the search for the Philosopher's Stone and the production of gold from base metals was an enormous task. However, all this multitude of substances and technologies from the arsenal of alchemy reveals only the physical and material side of the process. Specialised literature contains almost no mention of the spiritual transformation.

What were the raw materials, formulae and processes which accompanied the discovery of the spiritual Philosopher's Stone and achieving spiritual perfection? Considering the multitude of methods and procedures connected with the material quest, they must have used the same approach to mental evolution. What did they mix and what did they use for mental transformation?

How and what did they heat, cool and turn to steam?

TWENTY-SEVEN

Mental Transmutation

If the Universal is Mental in its nature, then Mental Transmutation must be the art of CHANGING THE CONDITIONS OF THE UNIVERSE, along the lines of Matter, Force and Mind.
— THE THREE INITIATES

What is a transmutation? The term is normally used to explain the transformation of base metals into gold. However, it can also be used to refer to the transformation of one nature, form or substance into another. When we talk about mental transmutation, we are entering the territory of what we call the "*Art of Mental Chemistry*".

Here transformations are made from one mental state to another. The elements used by the mental alchemist possess a different nature and quality. Although the thoughts, feelings, emotions differ from those of metals and elements, they all share the common property, "*to be transmuted from state to state; degree to degree; condition to condition; pole to pole; vibration to vibration*".

This quote from *The Kybalion* once again gives us good reason to think of rhythm or vibration, as the major driving factor in the "heat treatment" of elements. In other words heating, cooling and vaporization is effectuated by rhythmic features such as Tempo, Dynamics, Pitch and their various properties. This will be discussed later in the book in more detail.

According to ancient Hermetic Philosophy, "*The Principle of rhythm manifests on the Mental Plane as well as on the Physical Plane, and the bewildering succession of moods, feelings, emotions, and other mental states, are due to the backward and forward swing of the mental pendulum, which carries us from one extreme of feeling to the other.*" In other words, the expression of our emotions and behaviours is based on the speed, intensity, timbre and pitch of the voice of "the mental metronome".

This affects people, their actions and everything else that may be around them. We can assume that if we master the knowledge of the mental pendulum and the synchronization of positive vibrations while maintaining the right balance, we can find the path to the spiritual Philosopher's Stone. First we must find out more about the process and the elements of alchemy. How can we combine them? How can we heat them? To what temperature? And many other questions which are metaphorically focused on our mental transformation. We need a mental *"Periodic Table"*, to help us attain a basic understanding of the mental elements and how they are transmuted.

As I have already noted several times in this book, detailed and clear descriptions are difficult, even impossible to find. Here are a few examples from the *Kybalion*:

> "The student and practitioner of Mental Transmutation works among the Mental Plane, transmuting mental conditions, states, etc., into others, according to the various formulas, more or less efficacious", *or* "One may change his mental vibrations by an effort of Will, in the direction of deliberately fixing the Attention upon a more desirable state. Will directs the Attention, and Attention changes the Vibration. Cultivate the Art of Attention, by means of the Will, and you have solved the secret of the Mastery of Moods and Mental States."

Once again in the first excerpt, we are given general information without any clarity about these formulae. It is clear in the second quotation that there is no quality characteristic of *"the mental vibrations"*. Here, however, we are given wise advice with regard to the process of mental transmutation, shaped by the new Trinity (WILL - ATTENTION – MASTERY OF MOODS AND MENTAL STATES). I will call it THE TRIANGLE OF WILLING ATTENTION and will use this term to unify these three steps.

The ability to focus your mind for an unlimited period of time is achieved by a great power of Will. This process is very similar to meditation. It may sound paradoxical since we usually associate Will with behaviours arising from different forces which create conflict: in other words, tension. In the world of meditation we have to melt our egos and deeply immerse ourselves in the sense of timelessness. From this state our Will can function effortlessly thus directing our Attention.

In the previous chapter we saw that in the search for the Philosopher's Stone, the alchemists subjected various raw materials to *"complex and lengthy processes"*. It is reasonable to assume that in order to hone the skills required for the Triangle of the Willing Attention, and to reach higher mastery also requires tireless work and dedication. This ability should become second nature and needs to be turned on/off effortlessly and flawlessly implemented. To achieve this level requires prolonged practice and must be built on a basic understanding of the process and the mental elements.

In the next few chapters I will present the necessary background information which we will apply later to the practical mastery of mental transmutation. By changing our vibrations to positive ones and finding inner happiness, we can influence and change the vibrations around us.

TWENTY-EIGHT

From Aristotle to Geber

All that we possess by nature, we receive at the beginning as an opportunity, and later accomplish into reality.
— ARISTOTLE

Socrates taught us that once you know the truth, you will not lose it. To Aristotle, however, knowledge alone does not make people virtuous. To achieve high goals, one must work upon one's character. Aristotle also taught us that man is what he learns and develops in himself through his constant deeds. In this sense we must combat those excessive and affective reactions which prevent us from correct thinking and deeds. The best way of response is achieved through persistent and systematic training. The specific principles of Aristotle's philosophy led me to continue my research in the footsteps of his tradition.

In the last chapter, I concluded that it requires *"tireless work and dedication"* to master the Triangle of Willing Attention. This precious seed which is inherent in us needs to be cultivated and harvested carefully, in order that its beauty and elegance might truly shine. It is like shaping clay, sculpting stone, or forging iron into beautiful shapes and ornaments. The conversion of a primary state into something bearing the marks of nobility and perfection requires more effort and diligence than acts of degradation and destruction.

Possessed by the desire for change and transformation, Aristotle became a role model for other alchemists. This fact is important if we are to understand the detailed steps to transmutation, or at least a clue to this path. Aristotle's reputation among alchemists was due to his theory of the elements and how they change. His doctrine of *"prime matter"* played a crucial role in the development of ancient art. He considered prime matter to be the foundation of the material world, albeit intangible and untouchable. Although prime matter does not physically exist by itself, it can acquire physical dimensions and features at different stages of its form.

The first stage of the form is related to the four classical elements: EARTH, WATER, AIR, FIRE, and their characteristic properties. Each element is distinguished from and associated with one of the others according to four basic qualities of HOT, COLD, DRY and WET. Each of the elements is characterized by two qualities, one of which is dominant:

>EARTH – cold and dry (dominant)
>WATER – wet and cold (dominant)
>AIR – hot and wet (dominant)
>FIRE – dry and hot (dominant)

The following chart shows the relationship between elements:

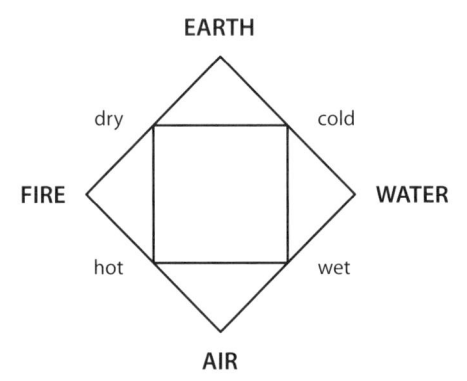

FIGURE 35

According to Aristotle each element can be transformed into the others by means of common qualities. For example, Earth may become Fire as a result of drought; Fire can be transformed into Air by heat; Air into Water through humidity; Water into Earth through cold. To make this process more visual, I have drawn lines to connect the qualities of dry - wet and hot - cold:

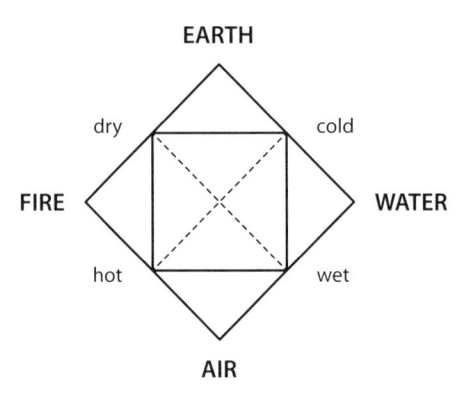

FIGURE 36

The line connecting wet and dry divides the square of two triangles, the vertices of which are common qualities of the elements:

Cold – WATER & EARTH
Hot – FIRE & AIR

WATER can change into EARTH, and FIRE into AIR, when dry and wet exchange positions, while retaining their common qualities, cold and hot, on the same vertices. A similar division can be done with the other pairs of elements: EARTH & FIRE, and AIR & WATER. This is achieved by uniting cold and hot features and reconfiguring two new triangles. The vertices contain common qualities of the elements – dry for the first pair, and wet for the second. EARTH can turn into FIRE, and AIR into WATER, while retaining their common qualities of dry and wet while hot and cold swap places.

According to this theory each element can perform a successive transmutation circle and then go back to the starting point; WATER can turn to EARTH; EARTH to FIRE; FIRE to AIR; and AIR again to WATER. It is important to note that through all these transformations, the prime matter located behind the form remains unchanged.

Aristotle believed that the next stage of form is related to all the natural phenomena in the world made of the four elements in different proportions, or as the Hermetics say, "*different levels of vibration*".

Aristotle's theories were particularly influential for Abū Mūsā Jābir ibn Ḥayyān, one of the most revered Arabian alchemists and Hermetics in the Western World, also known as Geber. Although we have no detailed information about his life, he is believed to have written over five hundred works devoted to the Philosopher's Stone.

In the 8th century (1,000 years after Aristotle), Geber borrowed from Aristotle's theories of prime matter and developed them in another direction. According to Geber, there are four primary natures: heat, cold, dryness and humidity. When these "*natures*" are combined with substance they produce compounds of the first degree: hot, cold, dry and wet. By combining the compounds they produce FIRE (hot + dry + substance), AIR (hot + wet + substance), WATER (cold + wet + substance) and EARTH (cold + dry + substance). The elements and their compounds, as determined by Geber, outline the forms we have already looked at in previous chapters:

FIGURE 37

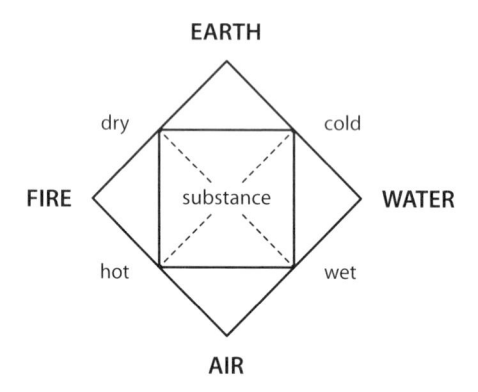

FIGURE 38

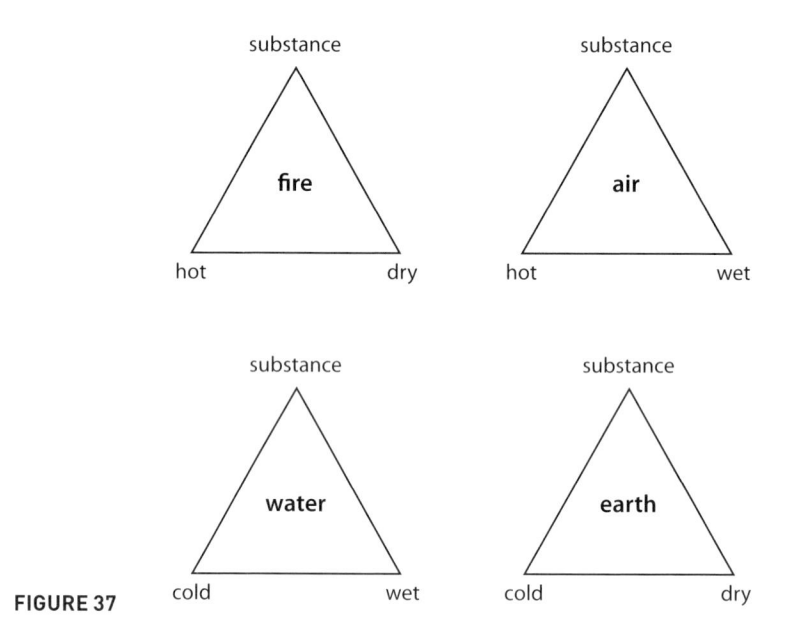

The difference here is the presence of a third element (substance) which lies inside the apex of the triangle. The trinities obtained can be summarized in the figure related to Aristotle's theory which was mentioned earlier:

Looking closely at the illustration, we can see that by folding the external triangles FIRE, AIR, WATER and EARTH into the centre, a pyramid is obtained (seen from above) with a common vertex, representing SUBSTANCE. This diagram shows the expanded and collected pyramid combining the theories of Aristotle and Geber in one. This pyramid, or capstone, takes us closer to my theory which I will introduce to you soon.

TWENTY-NINE

The Initiation Process

Whoso shall pass along this road alone, and without looking back, shall be purified by FIRE, WATER and AIR; and overcoming the fear of death, shall issue from the bowels of the EARTH to the light of day, preparing his soul to receive the mysteries of Isis.
— CHARLES WILLIAM HECKETHORN

We have seen how the theories of Aristotle and Geber were materialized in the Pyramid and Capstone of ancient knowledge. In search of a starting point for the process of mental transmutation, we find ourselves, once again, on the path of Trinities, triangles and pyramids. We can add new information to the previously discussed concept of the triangle enclosed in a circle and then summarize everything in a more complete scheme:

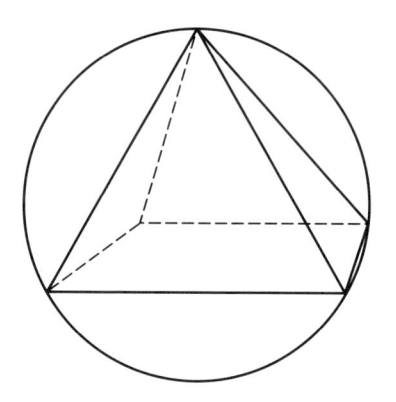

FIGURE 39

This drawing shows the pyramid made up of classic elements as well as the features of the elements and the cyclic transformation from one to another. It also shows the micro-macrocosmic concept of the nature of the Trinities; the Tetractys; and the numbers 3, 9, 13 and 27. We can thus see that not only do they exist as a whole, but they are also fundamental to physical and mental transmutation.

The pyramid is undoubtedly the key to achieving spiritual perfection and discovering the Philosopher's Stone. Few have reached these spiritual heights. Among them are Orpheus, Pythagoras and Plato who achieved great wisdom and mental strength through ritual initiation. They have been known since ancient times as *The Initiates*. You may not be surprised to learn that the process of initiation was held in the Great Pyramid at Giza.

Thomas Taylor, the famous Neo-Platonist described the details of Plato's initiation:

> Plato was initiated into the 'Greater Mysteries' at the age of 49. The initiation took place in one of the subterranean halls of the Great Pyramid in Egypt. The ISIAC TABLE formed the altar, before which the Divine Plato stood and received that which was always his, but which the ceremony of the Mysteries enkindled and brought from its dormant state. With this ascent, after three days in the Great Hall, he was received by the Hierophant of the Pyramid (the Hierophant was seen only by those who had passed the three days, the three degrees, the three dimensions) and given verbally the Highest Esoteric Teachings, each accompanied with its appropriate Symbol. After a further three months' sojourn in the halls of the Pyramid, the Initiate Plato was sent out into the world to do the work of the Great Order, as Pythagoras and Orpheus had been before him.

This quote refers to three facts which have already been mentioned in this book namely:

- "*The initiation took place in one of the subterranean halls of the Great Pyramid in Egypt.*" The alchemical process of mental transmutation is achieved with the help of the Great Pyramid, a monument built by Toth - Hermes Trismegistus.
- "*…before which the Divine Plato stood and received that which was always his, but which the ceremony of the Mysteries enkindled and brought from its dormant state.*" The confirmation that wisdom, truth and happiness sleep within us waiting to be awakened.
- "*…the Hierophant was seen only by those who had passed the three days, the three degrees, the three dimensions.*" Once again we come to the number 27, and respectively 9, in an already familiar way:

3 days x 3 degrees x 3 dimensions = 27 = 2 + 7 = 9

In order to be initiated into the secret teaching and to pass the test of alchemical transformation, the candidate needs to achieve the mathematical magnitude of 9 – the number of Man and the pyramid (as it symbolizes Man).

Fernando Malkun, the famous architect, researcher and explorer in the Mexican documentary *The Connection With Atlantis*, tells another ancient story:

> ...The pyramid is an ancient device used since the time of Atlantis, which has induced states of expanded consciousness through sound. The word "alchemy" is derived from "Chem" – the ancient name of Egypt. They say the alchemists are people who want to turn lead into gold, although alchemy in fact, is the search for enlightenment. The metal's transformation is just a by-product. The spiritualization of matter requires a high consciousness, presence in the very moment and use of inner energy.
>
> As a final step, in this transformational process the initiated used the Pyramid's three chambers. They spent *nine* days in them, inducing increasingly higher mental vibrations until they reached enlightenment. The students stayed in the underground chamber for three days, facing their fears and listening to their inner voices.
>
> The story tells there were different kinds of stones and crystals in the Grand Gallery of the pyramid. They were used as percussion instruments and their tones were associated with *three* musical scales. These majestic sounds deeply penetrated throughout the pyramid.
>
> In the second chamber, called the King's chamber, was located a large coffin made out of a single rock – a hard red granite. If we try to make that coffin today, we will need power drills with diamond tips which definitely were not available in 1500 BC. All this reveals a very deep mathematical knowledge. The outer volume of the coffin is exactly two times bigger than the inner one. The cubic size is similar to the Ark of the Covenant. Percussive strokes over its surface caused sounds which reverberated throughout the pyramid.
>
> It seems it was specifically designed to create high-frequency sounds, or electro-acoustic signals with an unknown technology. The story tells that the student stayed in that coffin for *three* days. He was a receiver of the echo of increasingly high sounds. The vibrations passed through the coffin and landed in the body, leading the candidate to higher levels of consciousness.

> In the so-called Queen's Chamber, the initiated remained for three more days. There he observed a transformed state of mind and the ability to change matter into spirit.

Once again there is the noticeable presence of the number three in the initiation ritual: 3 days in the Grand Gallery, 3 days in the King's Chamber and 3 days in the Queen's Chamber. Over a period of 9 days the candidate tests his will, power of concentration and ability to manage his mental emotions. These correspond to THE TRIANGLE OF WILLING ATTENTION which we have already discussed.

Malkun defines it perfectly in one sentence: "*The spiritualization of matter requires a high consciousness (Will), presence in the very moment (Attention) and the use of inner energy (Mastery of Moods and Mental States).*" A new fact stands out in this story in addition to the elements already known and the consistent confirmation of their application. This is SOUND and its application in the process of mental transmutation. The use of stones, crystals and the red granite coffin, made as percussion instruments, in order to produce a broad vibration spectrum that cause a higher level of consciousness, is the missing link in the conversion of matter into spirit.

Let us return to the discussion about Pakal's plaster heads found on the floor of his tomb. These statues represent the great ruler of the Mayans as a young boy and an old man. The main difference between them is that the figure of Pakal as an old man only has one ear. What could the reason for this be? Was his ear removed deliberately? Does it symbolize something? Is there a message? It is not the eye, nose or mouth which is missing, it is the ear. This is the organ through which we perceive sound vibrations in space.

The intentional omission of this organ in particular and the sum of 3 ears from two statues (again the number 3) leads me to think that it is intended to emphasize rather than to signify the lack of something important. It is a symbolism which draws attention to sound vibrations and their perception.

THIRTY

The Tablet of Isis

*The Tablet demonstrates that all is in God and God is in all;
that all is in all and each is in each.*
— *MANLEY PALMER HALL*

I would like to complete my historical journey with a short presentation and description of this ancient artefact which served as an altar before which the candidates for initiation would have stood. The tablet is known as the "Cardinal Bembo's Isiac Tablet", since after the pillage of Rome in 1527, it found its way into the hands of a blacksmith, who later sold it to Pietro Bembo, the Italian humanist, cardinal and academic.

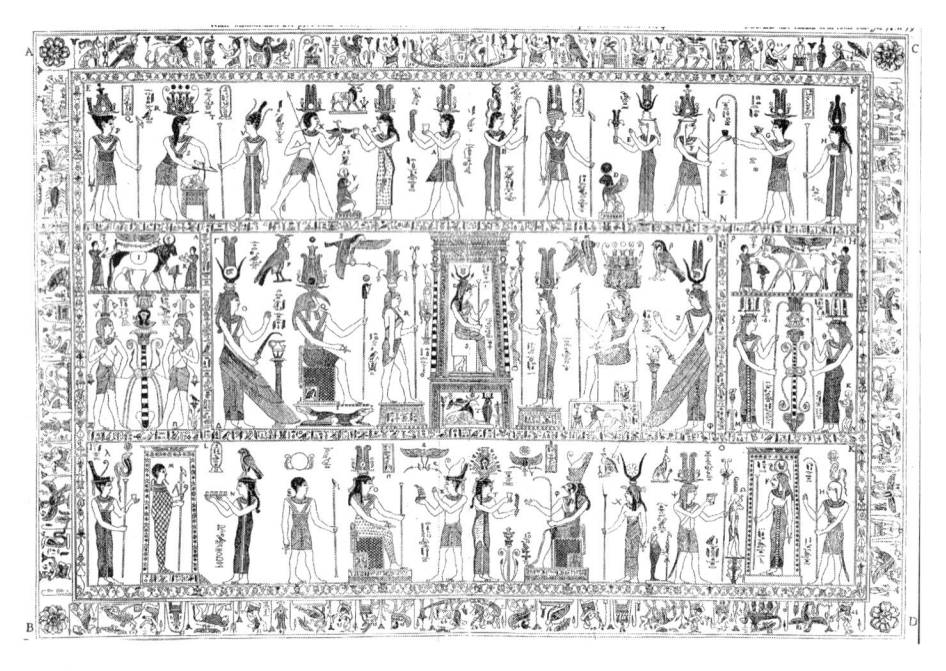

FIGURE 40

After his death it changed hands many times until it finally ended up in the Museum of Antiquities in Turin. The tablet was made of bronze and decorated with enamel with silver encrustations. Athanasius Kircher defined its parameters as four spans in width and five spans in length. Thomas Dudley Fosbrook, the English antiquary and researcher added:

> The figures are not deeply engraved and the contours of most of them are framed with silver threads. The base of the tablet was cast in silver and its left side, where there were no images, had clearly been broken off.

What exactly is the significance and what are its messages? Since ancient times the Egyptian oracles had tried to create a symbolic system which would express the essence of their secrete rituals. The Isiaic tablet contains their entire sacred knowledge, which is shown only to these who are admitted to the altar for initiation. The images upon it are believed to represent amulets which endow people with the virtues of Supreme Reason and protect them from evil. Kircher presents the symbolism of the tablet in his book *Oedipus of Egypt*, published in 1654, in the following way:

> It teaches, in the first place, the whole constitution of the threefold world –archetypal, intellectual, and sensible. The Supreme Divinity is shown moving from the centre to the circumference of a universe made up of both sensible and inanimate things, all of which are animated and agitated by the one supreme power which they call the Father Mind and represented by a threefold symbol. Here also are shown three triads from the Supreme One, each manifesting one attribute of the first Trimurti. These triads are called the Foundation, or the base of all things. In the Table is also set forth the arrangement and distribution of those divine creatures that aid the Father Mind in the control of the universe. Here [in the upper panel] are to be seen the Governors of the worlds, each with its fiery, ethereal, and material insignia. Here also [in the lower panel] are the Fathers of Fountains, whose duty it is to care for and preserve the principles of all things and sustain the inviolable laws of Nature. Here are the gods of the spheres and also those who wander from place to place, labouring with all substances and forms (Zonia and Azonia), grouped together as figures of both sexes, with their faces turned to their superior deity.

The book you are reading at the moment emphasizes the number of rhythm 3, its products 9 and 27, and the number 13. We have seen the enormous power and the meaning of the triunity and how it is set in the traditions, teachings and philosophers of the ancient sages. One of these was the great Zoroaster who said that the number three shines throughout the world. "Cardinal Bembo's Isiac Tablet" was created entirely on the basis of the triple principles and is further proof of this.

It is divided into three horizontal panels and can be said to represent the plan of the rooms in which the Mysteries of Isis were carried out. The central panel is divided into seven parts, or smaller rooms, and the image on the lower panel has a door on each side. The entire tablet contains forty-five images of primary significance and many more figures with less significance. The forty-five main figures are grouped into fifteen triads. Four of them are in the upper panel, seven are in the central panel and four can be seen in the lower panel of the Tablet.

In the original image the multitude of drawings and symbols can sometimes lead to confusion and difficulties in recognizing the triads. In 1887, Dr. William Winn Wescot [21] published a table in his book, *Cardinal Bembo's Isiac Tablet* which provides a visual representation of his key to the table.

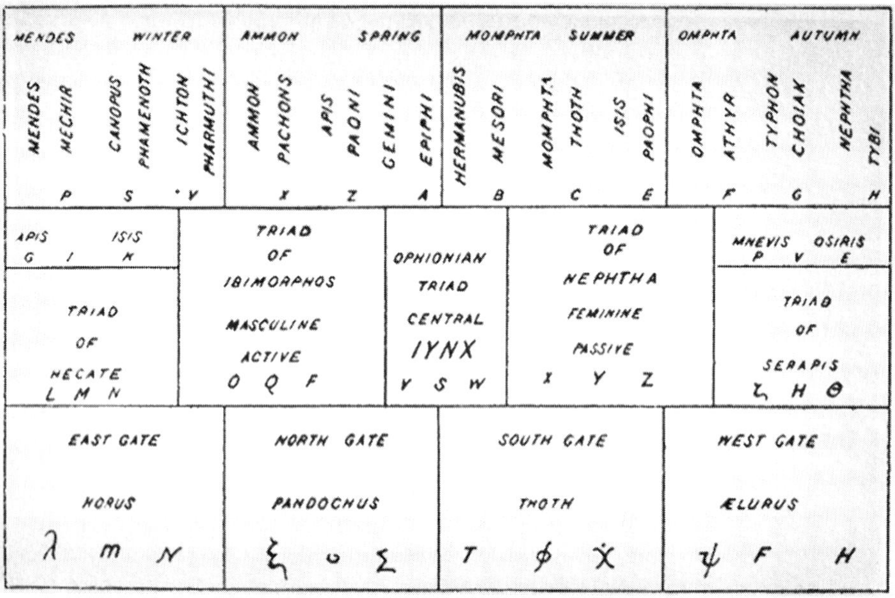

FIGURE 41

---

21 William Winn Westcot (1848 – 1925) – English occultist, one of the founders of the Hermetic Order of the Golden Dawn, the Supreme Magus of the Rosicrucian Society and Master of the Quator Coronati Lodge.

As we mentioned at the beginning of this chapter, the Isiac Tablet is clearly a huge subject and I don't want to go into detailed descriptions and analyses. For this reason we won't examine each one of the triads in every detail or the exact meaning of the letters connected with them. If you would like to examine this question in more detail, then I recommend the book by Manly Palmer Hall, *The Secret Teachings of All Times*.

The analysis which I would like to present to you is directly connected to the subject of my book and is connected with the table and numeric values. So let us look at the following:

Tablet panel	Number of triads	Total	Reduction	Final number and total (vertical)
1. Top	4	3+3+3+3=12	1+2	3
2. Middle	7	3+3+3+3+3+3+3=21	2+1	3
3. Bottom	4	3+3+3+3=12	1+2	3

FIGURE 42

The table, which I have created, demonstrates the absolute triple nature of the Isiaic Tablet. There are three panels and each one of them contains correspondingly 4 triads, 7 triads and once again 4 triads. The sum of each row is 12, 21 (anagram of 12) and 12. When we reduce the numbers, we obtain 3 threes in each panel. Since *"The Tablet demonstrates that all is in God and God is in all; that all is in all and each is in each"*, let us present this through the mathematical expression:

$$3 \times 3 \times 3 = 27 = 2 + 7 = 9$$

Once again we are witnesses to one and the same transformation of the rhythm number 3, which is clearly the main step in undertaking enlightenment and spiritual evolution.

The number of man/pyramid can be obtained in a simple way:

$$3 \times 15 \text{ triads} = 45 = 4+5 = 9$$

Athanasius Kircher describes the dimensions of the sides of the Isiaic Tablet as four spans and five spans (45). When the tablet was created, the span probably served as a unit of measurement and the ancients had encoded the sacred number 9 (4+5) not only in the number of triads, but also its dimensions.

All these thoughts and conclusions remind us of a table which I presented in the second part of the book (fig. 4). This table consisting of 45 cells unites the wisdom of Toth of Atlantis hidden in the "Emerald Tablets" and the structure of the Temple of the Inscriptions (the pyramid containing Pakal's tomb) in Palenque. We filled the empty cells with the artefacts discovered by Alberto Ruz Lhuillier and we discussed their symbolism and missive. We obtained the number 9 after numerological transformations. We can also observe the same thing in Cardinal Bembo's Isiac Tablet. I realize that all 45 members of the triads can fill the 45 empty cells of the above-mentioned table or simply be another addition to the All.

THIRTY-ONE

9

*At the current level of development
we live in a third dimension where the number 9
dominates above everything.*
— LINDA GOODMAN

Although we have already examined the number 9 and its symbolism in some detail, in this chapter I would like to pay a little more attention to it. I would, therefore, like to share some interesting and widely known facts about the number 9:

- When we add all the single digit numbers: 1+2+3+4+5+6+7+8+9, we obtain 45, which when we reduce it (4+5) we obtain 9.
- The number 9 cannot be destroyed, however much you multiply it, and this is not true for any other number. 9 multiplied by 2, makes 18 which when reduced (1+8) gives 9. Multiplied by 4 it gives 36 which when reduced (3+6) also produces the single-figure number 9, and so on until infinity.
- In astrology the harmonious aspects, or angles formed between the planets are: 30 degrees, 60 degrees and 120 degrees. Added together (or reduced) the numbers in them provide single-figure harmonious numbers 6 and 3. And the non-harmonious aspects or angles between the places which create tension are: 45 degrees, 90 degrees and 180 degrees, which reduced, makes 9.
- The Great Sidereal Year contains 25, 920 years. Summed up, the figures make 18 (2+5+9+2+0) which when reduced (1+8) makes 9. The sidereal year is closely connected with the Precession of Equinoxes – the time needed for all planets to return to their starting point. One degree of the procession takes 72 years. 7+2 is equal to 9. Two degrees of the procession take 144 years, three degrees take 216 years, five degrees take 360

years, while nine degrees take 720 years: added together the numbers are always equal to 9.
- During the 24-hour period we breathe on average 25,920 times; absolutely the same number as the number of years in the Great Sidereal Year!
- Women's pregnancy lasts 9 months.
- In one day there are 86,400 seconds which when added up makes 18, and this for its part, when reduced, adds up to 9.
- Normal breathing is 18 times per minute, and 1+8 equals 9.
- Normal pulse is 72 beats per minute. 7+2 is equal to 9.
- Normal hourly pulse is 4,320 – which also equals 9.
- We normally breathe 1,080 times every hour – 1+0+8+0= 9.
- In a 24-hour period, the heart beats 103, 680 times which when added again gives us 9.

Finally I would like to introduce the number 142 857, which has been considered "sacred" since the world began. According to the Kabbalah the number 142 857 contains the entire cosmic harmony. This unique number can be obtained by adding the symbol of Eternity – 0 – to the number 1. In this way we obtain 1, 000 000 or more. When we divide it by the mystical number 7 (embodying the spiritual side of things) we obtain 142 857.

$$1,000\,000 : 7 = 142\,857$$

We should note that however many zeros we add, if we continue to divide by 7 we will arrive at the same number. But why do we call it "sacred"? Similar to another sacred number (1, 366 560), which we have already looked at, when we add up the digits of 142 857 we arrive at the two digit number 27:

$$142\,857 = 1 + 4 + 2 + 8 + 5 + 7 = 27$$

If we add 2 and 7 (27 = 2+7) we obtain 9, the number of eternal energy and life in all its manifestations on the planet – the sacred number of Eternity.

THIRTY-TWO

The Matrix of the Capstone

*The Pyramid is an ancient time machine from
the era of the Atlanteans which used sound to invoke
conditions of expanded consciousness.*
— FERNANDO MALKUN

Our journey is heading towards its culmination point. We will soon be introduced to a matrix which contains everything which we have discussed in this book up to this point: Toth – Hermes Trismegistus' tablets, the architecture of the ancient Mayan and Egyptian pyramids, the sacred artefacts, the concept of micro and macro cosmos, Orpheus' lyre, the philosophy of Pythagoras, the teachings of Aristotle and Geber, the numbers 3, 9, 13, 27 and everything which is refracted through the vibrations, sound and language of rhythm.

As we have already seen, each one of these elements participates in the ritual of initiation, which in itself represents an alchemical process of spiritual enlightenment. For understandable reasons it is impossible today to reproduce exactly what took place in the halls of the Great Pyramid thousands of years ago, but we can get as close as possible by creating a virtual interactive model.

What is this model actually based upon and why is it virtual?

Since we cannot physically or actively stand inside the pyramid, we need to construct it virtually in our minds and create the conditions in which we can freely manipulate the elements of the transformational process. Since we are talking about mental transformation, these elements will not have a material essence, but a vibrational and sound nature which affects our emotions. Our "capstone" will not be created of stone but from invisible vibrating particles, which cannot be touched or seen in the way we are normally used to.

The key to their correct perception and realization is the Triangle of Willing Attention (Will – Attention – Mastery of Moods and Mental States), through which you will become transformed into alchemists and you will be able to change yourself and others. Up to this moment I have expressed most of the concepts in this book as numbers and tables and, therefore, I intend to present this Virtual Interactive Matrix in the same way. However, at the same time, it will create a multi-dimensional picture in your minds.

In the next few chapters I will successively analyse the details of my alchemical model, and then I will present the entire matrix.

THIRTY-THREE

3 x 3 x 3 (length)

My next step was to find further visual evidence. I had a good photograph of the three stars of Orion's Belt and was able to place it against the aerial shot of the three Giza pyramids. The correlation was stunning. Not only did the layout of the pyramids match the stars with uncanny precision but the intensity of the stars, shown by their apparent size, corresponded with the Giza group: there were three stars, three pyramids, three pharaohs Osiris-Orion kings.
— ROBERT BAUVAL

Triple triads (3 x 3 x 3) is perhaps the most frequently recurring pattern in cosmic geometry, ancient architecture, artefacts and rituals. We first discussed it in the concept of micro-macrocosm. Moving from top to bottom on the scale of manifestation, we came to vibration or rhythm, its three features Tempo, Dynamics, Pitch and their three Trinities:

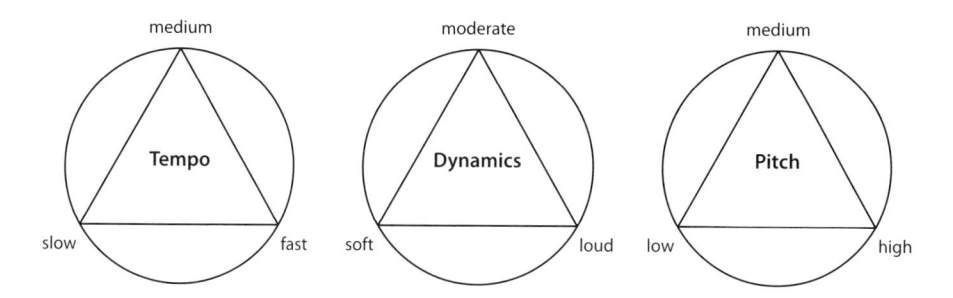

FIGURE 43

Following the model, 3 (slow, medium, fast) x 3 (soft, moderate, loud) x 3 (low, medium, high) = 27 permutations (see table below). You can listen to these patterns on the CD which is included with this book.

RHYTHM ALCHEMY

	Rhythm / Sound Patterns
1.	soft dynamics - fast tempo - high pitch
2.	moderate dynamics - slow tempo - high pitch
3.	moderate dynamics - slow tempo - medium pitch
4.	moderate dynamics - fast tempo - high pitch
5.	loud dynamics - slow tempo - low pitch
6.	moderate dynamics - medium tempo - high pitch
7.	soft dynamics - fast tempo - medium pitch
8.	soft dynamics - slow tempo - medium pitch
9.	soft dynamics - fast tempo - low pitch
10.	moderate dynamics - slow tempo - low pitch
11.	soft dynamics - medium tempo - medium pitch
12.	loud dynamics - medium tempo - low pitch
13.	soft dynamics - slow tempo - low pitch
14.	loud dynamics - fast tempo - low pitch
15.	moderate dynamics - fast tempo - medium pitch
16.	loud dynamics - fast tempo - medium pitch
17.	moderate dynamics - medium tempo - medium pitch
18.	loud dynamics - medium tempo - medium pitch
19.	soft dynamics - slow tempo - high pitch
20.	moderate dynamics - fast tempo - low pitch
21.	loud dynamics - fast tempo - high pitch
22.	loud dynamics - slow tempo - medium pitch
23.	soft dynamics - medium tempo - high pitch
24.	loud dynamics - slow tempo - high pitch
25.	loud dynamics - medium tempo - high pitch
26.	soft dynamics - medium tempo - low pitch
27.	moderate dynamics - medium tempo - low pitch

FIGURE 44

These 27 patterns represent all the possible combinations of nine elements of Tempo, Dynamics and Pitch and are listed in random order. Each of these 27 models creates sonic vibrations with different characteristics and intensity in space.

These rhythmic oscillations lie at the very heart of creation and manifestation of the living universe. The Hermetic "*Principle of Correspondence*" and "*Principle of Rhythm*" resonate in each of these sounds. What is "*above*" is reflected in what is found "*below*" and vice versa – what is "*below*" is in what is "*above*" through the tireless dance of vibrations. Everything moves and vibrates in a united rhythm of The All.

These sounds must have washed over the candidates as they went through their initiation.

In the column and its content we can also find Pythagoras' Tetractys which I developed in more detail in the previous chapters:

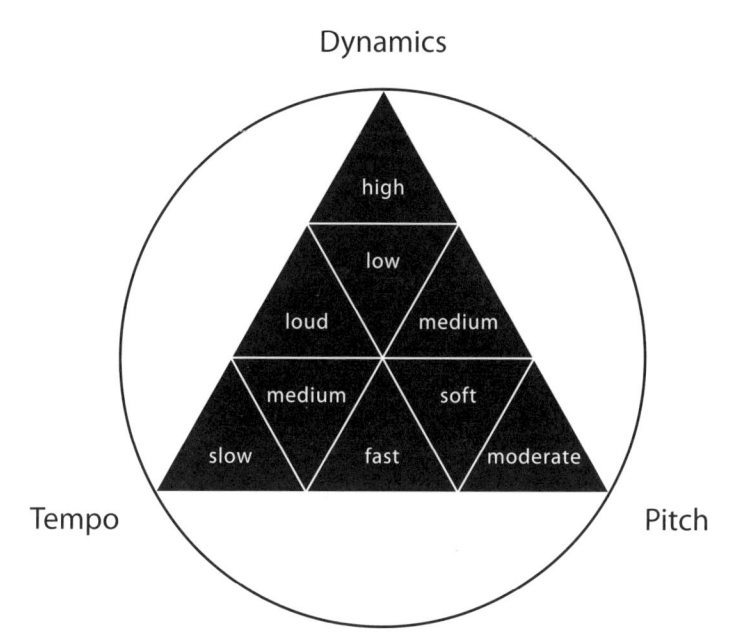

FIGURE 45

The circle surrounding the Tetractys symbolizes the cyclical movement of rhythms/vibrations and The All in which all elements of the micro-macrocosmic scale can be found.

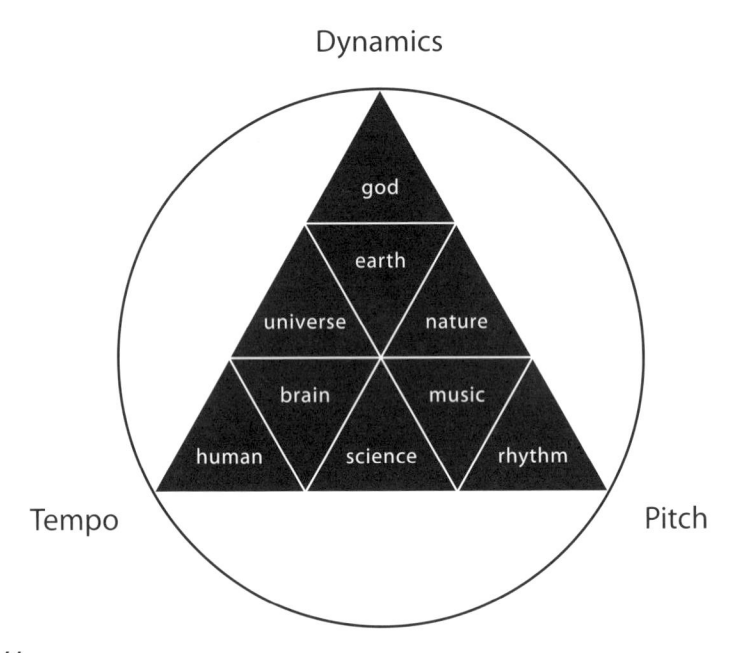

FIGURE 46

The theories and teachings of Aristotle and Geber contain useful information about the process of physical transmutation; using the properties of the elements EARTH – WATER – AIR – FIRE. While Aristotle uses two of the properties of the elements for their alchemical change, Geber includes one other: substance. The conversion of one element into another is achieved through their common qualities. It can be said that the various transformational formulae were developed using their permutations.

Exactly the same processes happen in my Table – all 27 permutations were developed by 9 features and their ternary combinations.

At this developmental stage of the Virtual Interactive Matrix I asked myself the question, "*Well, I have the properties, I combined them, but what in fact are the elements?*" At that moment I realized that the "*elements*" such as Tempo, Dynamics and Pitch, which I have used, cannot be defined as such. Rather they perform the function of "*cause*" – the basis for the generation of vibrations with such specific properties. However, the real elements were still missing from the overall system which I was trying to create.

In a similar way in which the prime matter elements are involved in material transmutation, the elements of mental transmutation are necessary to reflect the nature of our mental and emotional states. Defining these psychological conditions is a necessary step in the process of constructing this model.

Earlier I presented and analysed the vertical part of the table, now let us look at the horizontal.

THIRTY-FOUR

13 (width)

The number 13 is not a fatal one, as many people believe. In ancient times, they claimed that "somebody who knows how to use the number 13 will obtain force and power."
— *LINDA GOODMAN*

Sounds born from the combination of the nine properties create vibrations in air. Their rhythmic characteristics then establish the various types of emotions. Namely those emotions are the mental elements which will form the horizontal plane of the Virtual Interactive Matrix and will actively participate in the transmutation process.

Here, two very important questions arise. Which emotions should I use? What are the main criteria for their selection? It would clearly be overwhelmingly impossible to use all the alternatives. Therefore, I first determine the number of emotions and the specific criteria for their inclusion. In the charts so far, special attention has been paid to another very important number.

It is now time to include the number 13 – the symbol of United Rhythm. Although the number 13 can be seen as 1 (circle, unity) and 3 (rhythm) in the vertical plane of the matrix, its placement there seems different to the numbers 3, 9 and 27. This pattern can be seen horizontally and semi-horizontally in the Kukulkan pyramid in Chichen Itza – 13 triangles (7 white + 6 black); Orpheus' lyre – 13 filled and empty spaces (7 strings + 6 spaces); the Menorah – 13 filled and empty spaces (7 arms + 6 spaces).

However, this is not the only reason to use 13 kinds of emotions arranged horizontally. The symbolism of the number 13 in the above examples, such as night and day, black and white, inhalation and exhalation, creates rhythmic structure from which the desired emotions begin to emerge. Dr. Calleman's chart, which reflects the thirteen stages in the development of each of the nine time-cycles, is very helpful in determining this.

These stages are treated as seven days and six nights during which creative, destructive and fading processes take place. In other words these are periods of light and dark, or positive and negative emotions which accompany the evolution of consciousness. Let us recall the pattern of maturation which schematically represents all elements of the creative process:

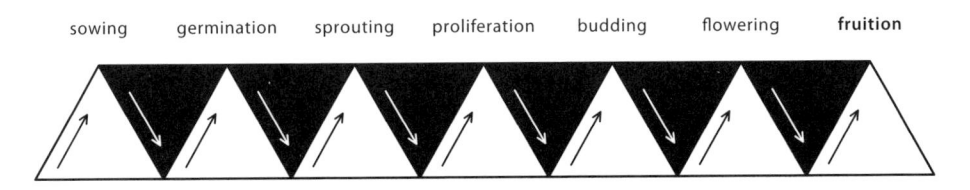

sowing   germination   sprouting   proliferation   budding   flowering   fruition

FIGURE 47

This series of black and white triangles form the basis for selecting the number and nature of the emotions listed in Figure 48. I incorporated the teachings of Zoroaster for the separation of light and darkness, the good and evil principle and positive and negative energies in this process. Among them I integrated several emotions which exist in the spectrum of the positive and the negative.

The mental transmutation, which we will now focus our attention on, is the positive one. Therefore, all of these emotions which contain two connotations will be directed to the positive side. I was about to take the important step of selecting the specific emotions. My goal was to choose the most common examples which clearly demonstrate their opposites, for example: love - hate, anger - peace, etc. The number 13, the pattern of night and day, the entire Mayan mythology and that of the other civilizations of Central America which are built on the Thirteen Heavenly Kingdoms, reminded me of another important detail which brought an even greater sense of an emotional horizontal:

> Each one of the Thirteen Heavenly Kingdoms corresponds to certain evolutionary processes in time and dominant deity. The odd numbers of each of them are associated with divine light and day; the even numbers with darkness and night. The conclusion one can draw is that the seven odd and six even heavens are not something different than the seven days and six nights of God's creation.

This excerpt from Chapter 13 in Part Two, suggested to me that I could construct the emotions as they correspond to the nature of the deities. This is what we obtained:

13th Heavens	Deities	Emotions
1.	Xiuhtecuhtli: God of Fire and Time	Pride
2.	Tlaltecuhtli: God of the Earth	Sorrow
3.	Chalchiuhtlicue: Goddess of Water	Peace
4.	Tonatiuh: God of the Sun and Warriors	Courage
5.	Tlacoteotl: Goddess of Love and Childbirth	Love
6.	Mictlantecuhtli: God of Death	Fear
7.	Cinteotl: God of Maize and Sustenance	Neutrality
8.	Tlaloc: God of Rain and War	Anger
9.	Quetzalcoatl: God of Light	Hope
10.	Tezcatlipoca: God of Darkness	Hatred
11.	Yohualticitl: Goddess of Birth	Joy
12.	Tlahuizcalpantecuhtli: God before Dawn	Guilt/Shame
13.	Ometeotl/Omecinatl: Dual-Creator God	Happiness

FIGURE 48

NOTE: The elements of mental transmutation (emotions) from the original matrix will be listed horizontally. Here they are placed vertically for clarity.

At first glance, perhaps some of the suggested pairings do not seem obvious. However, at a deeper level of awareness there are very close analogies. The odd numbers (years) denote the stages of development and interestingly they represent the cycles of *"female"* energy. The even numbers (years) are represented by the deities associated more often with the *"male"* energies of death destruction and war. This aspect of cycling can be seen as a time for rest in the odd-numbered heavens; and a time for new things and actions in the even-numbered ones.

In this context, and with minor clarifications which I will add later, it is logical to say that positive emotions are represented by odd numbers, while negative emotions are represented by even numbers. *"Neutrality"*, lies in the centre of the table. It presents the idea of a balance between conflicting emotions. This balance may again be represented by a triangle and/or pyramid. This is the Trinity of Deity no. 1 – Xiuhtecuhtli; Deity no. 7 – Cinteotl; Deity no. 13 – The Dual-Creator God Ometeotl/Omecinatl.

```
              Cinteotl,
       god of maize and sustenance
                  /\
                 /  \
                /    \
               /      \
              /        \
             /          \
            /_____\
   Xiuhtecuhtli,        Ometeotl/Omecinatl,
 god of fire and time    Dual - Creator God
```

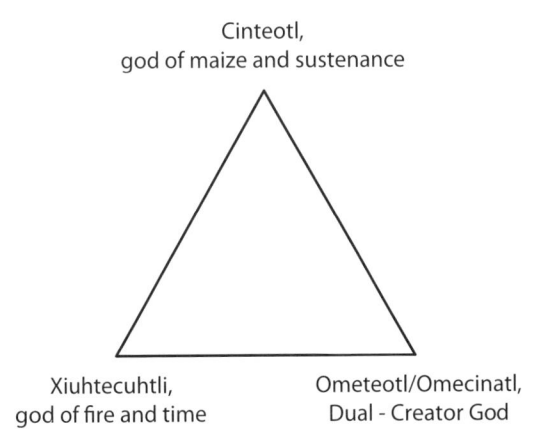

FIGURE 49

This complete emotional range can be represented as a seven-storey pyramid, upon the peak of which the mental elements are balanced. It thus shows us the intricacies of successful alchemical transmutation:

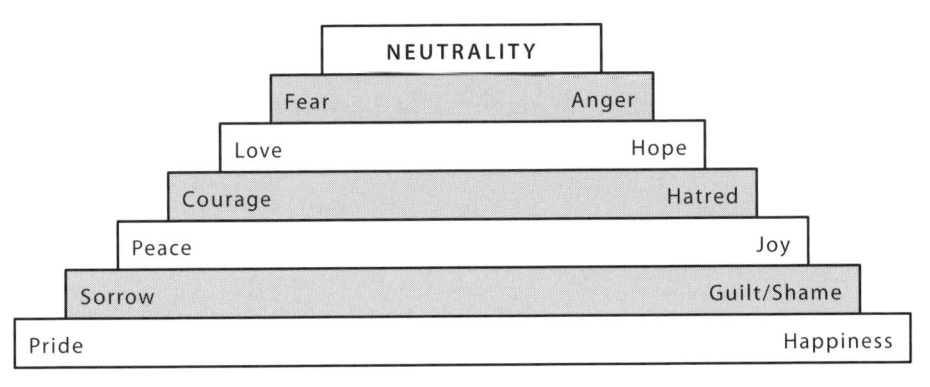

```
                NEUTRALITY
          Fear              Anger
       Love                    Hope
     Courage                     Hatred
   Peace                            Joy
  Sorrow                            Guilt/Shame
 Pride                                Happiness
```

FIGURE 50

In this pyramid of emotions we can clearly see the expression of the other two Hermetic principles: *"The Principle of Polarity"* and *"The Principle of Gender"*. The dual nature of each manifestation in the Cosmos appears as two opposing aspects of the EMOTION element. The Male and Female principles which bear the properties of gender pulsate at a physical, mental and spiritual level.

It is time to expand our table and enter more deeply into the essence of the Virtual Interactive Matrix.

THIRTY-FIVE

The Virtual Interactive Matrix

On the next page I will show you the completed table. However, let us first consider in detail how it is used, and once more summarize everything contained therein.

- The Great Pyramid
- The Pyramid of Chichen Itza
- The Temple of the Inscriptions in Palenque
- The Seven Hermetic Principles
- Orpheus' Lyre
- Pythagoras' Tetractys
- The Alchemy of Aristotle and Geber
- Isis's tablet
- The Great Number of synthesis 1, 366 560
- Mayan mythology
- The numbers 3, 9, 13 and 27 etc.

All these components and many others which, due to their volume, we have not discussed in this book, form the basis of the model which we will use in our work to assimilate the process of mental transmutation. However, before we can run, we need to learn and crawl and then to walk. In order to learn to read and talk, we need to learn the alphabet, words and assimilate the skill of arranging them meaningfully in a sentence.

This is the function of the matrix which I will propose. It contains 27 sounds representing the spectrum of different emotional vibrations. Each one of these sounds has a specific frequency characteristic and possesses qualities typical of the letters of the alphabet which we all know. You may not easily recall the moments when you made your first efforts to patiently learn the alphabet, which we use today to write and talk, but if we want to use the language of emotions freely and without tension and to be able to change them, then we need to make the same efforts.

The entire process of achieving mental mastery is directly connected with the Triangle of Willing Attention. Thus, in order to master each one of the twenty-seven models/letters, we need to apply Will, Attention and Knowledge of our emotions. We shall encounter these details further on in the book, but let us first look at the Virtual Interactive Matrix. The total number of cells or "bricks" forming my Virtual Interactive Matrix can be calculated in the following way:

$$27 \times 13 = 351$$

If we reduce this numeric value we obtain:

$$351 = 3 + 5 + 1 = 9 - \text{The number which symbolizes man.}$$

	Rhythm/ sound models	PRIDE	SORROW	PEACE	COU
1.	Soft dynamics – fast tempo – high pitch				
2.	Moderate dynamics – slow tempo – high pitch				
3.	Moderate dynamics – slow tempo – medium pitch				
4.	Moderate dynamics – fast tempo – high pitch				
5.	Loud dynamics – slow tempo – low pitch				
6.	Moderate dynamics – medium tempo – high pitch				
7.	Soft dynamics – fast tempo – medium pitch				
8.	Soft dynamics – slow tempo – medium pitch				
9.	Soft dynamics – fast tempo – low pitch				
10.	Moderate dynamics – slow tempo – low pitch				
11.	Soft dynamics – medium tempo – medium pitch				
12.	Loud dynamics – medium tempo – low pitch				
13.	Soft dynamics – slow tempo – low pitch				
14.	Loud dynamics – fast tempo – low pitch				
15.	Moderate dynamics – fast tempo – medium pitch				
16.	Loud dynamics – fast tempo – medium pitch				
17.	Moderate dynamics – medium tempo – medium pitch				
18.	Loud dynamics – medium tempo – medium pitch				
19.	Soft dynamics – slow tempo – high pitch				
20.	Moderate dynamics – fast tempo – low pitch				
21.	Loud dynamics – fast tempo – high pitch				
22.	Loud dynamics – slow tempo – medium pitch				
23.	Soft dynamics – medium tempo – high pitch				
24.	Loud dynamics – slow tempo – high pitch				
25.	Loud dynamics – medium tempo – high pitch				
26.	Soft dynamics – medium tempo – low pitch				
27.	Moderate dynamics – medium tempo – low pitch				

Figure 51 The Matrix Table

THE VIRTUAL INTERACTIVE MATRIX

	Emotions and Energy							
E	FEAR	NEUTRALITY	ANGER	HOPE	HATRED	JOY	GUILT/SHAME	HAPPINESS

Now that the matrix has been completed, let us look at an interesting fact – both sides of the seal of the USA, which can be seen on the One dollar note. The great seal was created and used for the first time in 1782 by the mystical philosophers who founded the USA.

Clearly the enlightened fathers of the nation encoded the ancient symbols of the Mysteries in the seal. It seems to contain everything which we have discussed up to this present moment in this book, and we can see a similarity with the Virtual Interactive Matrix which I have shown above.

I should note that I discovered these similarities some time after I had created the matrix. Although I had seen the seal on a one-dollar note, I had never paid much attention to it, until I saw it depicted in a book. After reading a detailed analysis of the seal, I could not help but compare it with my model. So, if we look at the front:

FIGURE 52

The central figure is an eagle, but in fact, it is a stylized image of a phoenix, as can be seen in the original first version of the seal. According to mediaeval Hermetics, the phoenix is the symbol of the completion of alchemical transmutation. This is a process which can be compared with spiritual rebirth. It is the transformation or rebirth of creative energy, known in alchemy as the completion of the Great Creation.

I can boldly say that the symbolism of the bird is the basic motive for writing this book and presenting the interactive matrix which I created. Now look at the tail of the "eagle" and then the shield above it. Do you notice anything familiar? There are 9 tail feathers and 13 stripes upon the shield. These are the parameters of the Virtual Interactive Matrix along the vertical and horizontal axes. Furthermore, the stripes on the shield consist of 7 white and 6 black ones (7 days and 6 nights). As we have already mentioned this is the motive expressed in the manora, Orpheus' lyre and the pyramid at Chichen Itza.

Based on this concept I created the thirteen mental elements, which in fact consist of 7 positive and 6 negative emotions. In fact the mystical number of the Unified Rhythm – 13, exists everywhere on this side of the seal – 13 stripes on the shield, 13 arrows in the left claw, a branch with 13 leaves and 13 fruit in the right claw, and 13 stars above its head, 13 letters in the inscription "E pluribus unum" (From the many – one) on the strip in the beak. There are 6 repetitions of the number 13, or

$$6 \times 13 = 78$$
$$78 = 7 + 8 = 15$$
$$15 = 1 + 5 = 6$$

We obtain the number 6 which in fact is the inverted 9, in other words the parameters of the interactive matrix 9 and 13 can be seen in the complete picture of the front side of the seal.

Let us look at the opposite side:

FIGURE 53

The central figure here is the Egyptian pyramid, the capstone of which is separate and hanging in the air. Upon it is the mystical eye of Horus, the son of Isis and Osiris. The symbolism of this picture is one more synchronization with the pulsation of my intents. Whatever meaning its creators may have invested in this symbol, for me the separated capstone and the eye express the search of the lost stone – the Philosopher's Stone of Enlightenment.

Without it the pyramid is incomplete, as can be seen on the seal. It is remarkable that the incomplete pyramid has the same proportions – 9 and 13 – as my matrix. Note that there are 13 rows and that the number of stones on the façade of the pyramid, with the exception of the date panel, amounts to 72. Seventy two (72) is the anagram of 27 or 2 + 7 = 9 – the vertical axis of my model. It is as though the seal was saying to me, "Look for the enlightenment hidden in the incomplete pyramid!"

THIRTY-SIX

Cause and Effect – 1st level

Every Cause has its Effect; every Effect has its Cause.
— KYBALION

It is now time to breathe life into the Virtual Interactive Matrix. In order to start the mental alchemical process we need to apply the Hermetic principle of "*Cause and Effect*". The cause will be produced by the vibrations of the properties of the mental elements, and by means of the Triangle of Willing Attention we will materialize the effect of the emotions in our conscious minds.

After acquiring Knowledge of emotions through Will and Attention, we will obtain a response showing which properties relate to the corresponding mental elements. This will allow us to participate to the full in the alchemic transmutation which manifests itself in two areas:

- It causes a specific emotional condition.
- It transforms one emotion into another.

Only after we have constructed firm knowledge and abilities based upon the vibrational properties of the mental elements can we achieve emotional transformation. In other words, in order to create within ourselves or in other people a given emotion, and to learn how to change it, we need to define how it vibrates. This will be our first practical task.

You can listen to the patterns included on the CD with this book.

Now let us look at the rhythmic models. Each one of them possesses three of the properties of the mental elements which interest us. These properties are a combination of the characteristics of rhythm – Tempo, Pitch and Dynamics. Each model represents a cyclic repetition of 4 identical sounds with the corresponding characteristics. You might want to ask me why there are 4 sounds and not 2 or 3 for example? Since one of our basic aims is to construct a virtual sound model of the pyramid or its capstone in our minds, we need to create a feeling of volume.

We can only achieve this with the four triangular walls of the pyramid which are represented by the four repetitive pulsations of the recording.

This is what Dr. José Argüelles[22] writes about the Mayan calendar:

> ... but to return to the "calendar" and its numbers, as noted, in the 260- and 360- unit "calendars", we see the key numbers: 4, 9 and 13. 4 is the number signifying measure; 9 is the number signifying periodicity or completeness; 13 is the number signifying the movement immanent in all things. The difference between 9 and 13 is, of course, 4.

If we apply this knowledge to the Virtual Interactive Matrix we will see that it possesses the same key numbers, in which 13 is horizontal, 9 (27 = 2 + 7) – vertical, and the difference between – 4, represents the four triangular walls of the pyramid.

The number of mental emotional elements – 13 – also suggests the volume structure:

$$13 = 1 + 3 + = 4 \text{ walls in the Unified Cyclic Rhythm}$$

Each wall also symbolizes the points of the compass (East, South, West, North), the seasons (Spring, Summer, Autumn, Winter) and the elements (Air, Fire, Earth, Water).

Now we can build this model and experience the world of emotional vibrations. Be patient and be prepared to concentrate. Without looking at the matrix presented above, take some blanks sheets of paper and a pencil. Find a quiet, dimly lit and well-aired room where you can listen to the recording on the compact disc on headphones. Establish the real compass points of the earth and place yourself comfortably in the centre of this imagined square where the base of the pyramid will be.

You will probably recognise this scheme, since it is almost identical with that of Aristotle and Geber with slight changes. Since the most ancient of times philosophers have made comparisons between the primary elements and man. Rocks and soil correspond to bones and flesh, air to the gases in the human body, water to bodily fluids and fire to body temperature. We are now in the centre of this interactive scheme in which we will undertake our mental transformations.

Depending on your desire and your mood, look in one of the directions so that the back of your head and your shoulders are pointing in the other three directions.

---

22 Dr. José Argüelles (1939 – 2011) – American historian who devoted his entire life to studying the civilization of the Mayans.

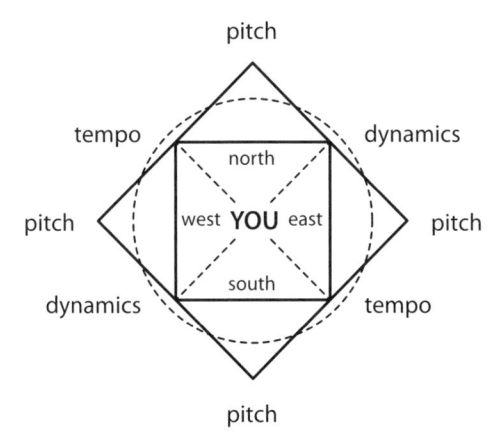

FIGURE 54

Close your eyes and breathe in deeply, hold your breath and slowly breathe out. Continue the cycle of slow and rhythmic breathing in and out, until you gradually achieve a state of relaxation. Slowly reach out and turn on the recording. When you hear the first vibration model, try without making too much effort to recognise the four tones which repeat in a cycle. Each one of these represents a triangular wall of the pyramid constructed from three factors – Tempo, Dynamics and Pitch. (fig. 54).

Set yourself the task of synchronizing each sound with each wall in a clockwise direction. Do it in such a way that they form the pyramid in your mind. The walls and sounds surround you with their cyclical movement, and the top of your head forms the peak of the pyramid. Begin with the imagined triangle in front of you, then from your right hand, the back of your head and your left hand. You need to visualize the walls in synchronicity with each sound and try to concentrate on this process as long as possible without too much effort.

This is the moment where you need actively to apply the concept of the Triangle of Willing Attention. When you feel any tension and difficulty in continuing, stop the aural and visual construction of the triangular walls, relax again and go back to the former state of relaxation. Now imagine that you are surrounded by the entire pyramid and direct your attention to the characteristics of the rhythm. What is the tempo? Fast, slow or medium? What is the pitch of the sounds? Low, medium or high? What are the dynamics of the strength? Soft, moderate or loud?

Carefully think about the model and its rhythmic characteristics. When you are sure that you can define the model, slowly open your eyes, take the pencil, draw a triangle and next to each of the tips, write what you can hear in terms of tempo, pitch and dynamics. Repeat the same exercise with each of the other 26 models. When you have finished, compare what you have written with the vertical axis of the Virtual Interactive Matrix, which you can see in the previous chapter.

In order to pass onto the next level in mastering the necessary skills, you must not have made a mistake in defining the properties of the models. If you have made any mistakes, then work upon the problematic areas in the way I described above. When you feel ready, set up your CD player to replay the models in a random order, or ask someone to play them to you in a random order. This time you do not need to repeat the entire meditational procedure, but you need to be calm, relaxed and able to identify the corresponding model.

The aim at the first level is to achieve mastery in recognizing each rhythmic model without effort and with the aid of the Triangle of Willing Attention. If you have completed the exercise without making any mistakes in defining tempo, dynamics and pitch for each one of the models then we can pass onto the next level.

THIRTY-SEVEN

Correlation – 2nd level

When the wind blows, listen to the sound.
— *PYTHAGORAS*

Now that we can easily define the different nuances of rhythm, we can now look for conformity between the properties and their emotions. In order to do this we need to repeat the same meditation of the first level, but to add two new elements. Instead of blank sheets of paper, make a copy of the Virtual Interactive Matrix and be prepared to use it. Work with each model individually, and make sure you control your breathing in accordance with the different tempos. The second level includes a number of steps which we need to follow:

STEP ONE
- From the level of deep relaxation, play the recording and begin to synchronize the sounds with the imagined triangular walls surrounding you and forming the pyramid with the peak at the top of your head. This time you do not need to think about the sounds. You need to be able to identify them immediately as one of the twenty seven "letters" of the alphabet of vibrations. You should not perceive the specific tempo, pitch and dynamics separately, but as a whole functioning as one single "letter".

STEP TWO
- Gradually include rhythmic breathing into the overall synchronicity. This consists of 4 pulses of breathing in and 4 pulses of breathing out, or a cycle of two rotations of the circle:

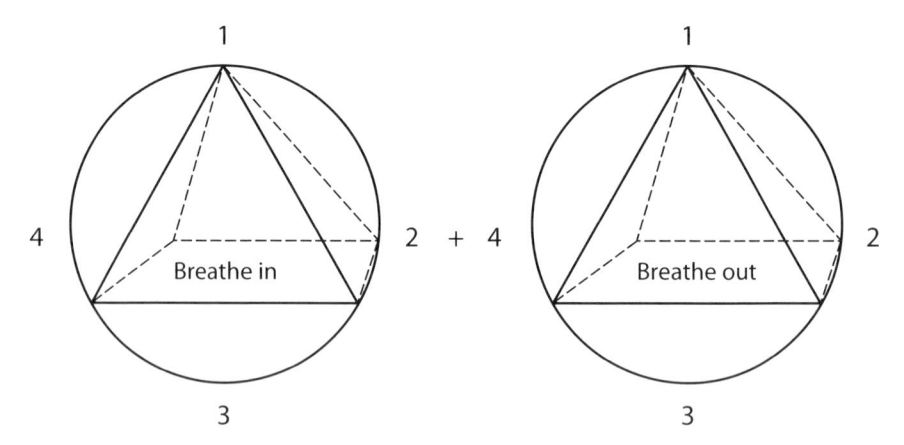

FIGURE 55

Depending on the change in the tempo of the rhythm models, the tempo of breathing changes as well. Here are a few additional recommendations which would make this step easier and will contribute to the better mastery of these skills:

- With the slower tempos, breathe in through the nose and out through the mouth, while slightly emphasizing each pulse. After a while when you feel comfortable with this addition, the breathing out should be accompanied with a sound which conforms to the pitch/loudness of the tone on the recording. Use the vowel sounds A, E, I, O, or U at your discretion and in this way you will be able to cause vibrations in every cell of your body. As a result of these vibrations, the cells will begin to synchronize with each other. We will also achieve synchronicity at another level of the exercise.
- Observe the same instructions with the moderate tempos.
- With faster tempos, breathe in through the nose and breathe out through the nose. Due to the fast changes in the 4-pulse cycle, the addition of emphases, and an additional sound when breathing out, might be too much of a challenge, so I recommend concentrating on the synchronization of breathing in and breathing out, and the sounds which you can hear.

NOTE: I recommend that you first practice each level of rhythmic models at a slow tempo, then those at a moderate tempo, and finally those at a fast tempo. In this way you will achieve a gradual gradation and accumulation of new knowledge and skills.

STEP THREE

The next stage is to add an element of rest and thought. In the table below I have listed the exercises which you need to carry out. They must all be carried out in the order indicated (1, 2, 3, and 4), in accordance with the tempos shown and without interruption:

	ACTION (breathing in – breathing out) Breathing in and breathing out accompanied by sound when possible!	**REST** (thought - compliance) In a state of complete rest, stop observing the corresponding rhythmic breathing and concentrate only on listening to the rhythmic models!
1.	Slow tempo – 1 cycle* – 8 pulses Moderate tempo – 2 cycles – 16 pulses Fast tempo – 4 cycles – 32 pulses	Slow tempo – 1 cycle* – 8 pulses Moderate tempo – 2 cycles – 16 pulses Fast tempo – 4 cycles – 32 pulses
2.	Slow tempo – 2 cycles – 16 pulses Moderate tempo – 4 cycles – 32 pulses Fast tempo – 8 cycles – 64 pulses	Slow tempo – 2 cycles – 16 pulses Moderate tempo – 4 cycles – 32 pulses Fast tempo – 8 cycles – 64 pulses
3.	Slow tempo – 4 cycles –32 pulses Moderate tempo – 8 cycles – 64 pulses Fast tempo – 16 cycles – 128 pulses	Slow tempo – 4 cycles – 32 pulses Moderate tempo – 8 cycles – 64 pulses Fast tempo – 16 cycles – 128 pulses
4.	Rest and listening & thought and compliance	

FIGURE 56

*One cycle refers to the succession of breathing in (4 pulses) and breathing out (4 pulses) = 8 pulses.

As you may have noticed, as we observe the succession of action and rest, we gradually enter more spatial time dimensions, until we eventually reach the stage of "timelessness". After measuring the relevant cycles of action and rest in exercise 3, in exercise 4 you stop counting, constructing the walls in your mind, breathing in accordance with the changes in tempo and synchronizing yourself with them.

In a state of deep rest gradually draw a picture of yourself in your mind. Imagine that you are outside your body and you are observing yourself from the side – sitting in the centre of the scheme shown above (fig. 54 and 55), surrounded by the triangular vibrating walls of the pyramid. Imagine that you are a pyramid. Your knees and your head form a triangle pulsating with the proportions of the pyramid – 9 (27) and 13. These proportions exist within us. Nine is the number of man and thirteen the number of the primary joints which connect our bodily parts.

Sense yourself relaxing more and more and remove the tension from the joint which connects your head with your body, the joints of your shoulders, your elbows, your wrists, your hips, knees and ankles. There are 13 joints in total, the same as the number of days and nights, and the same as the number of mental emotional elements. Take a deep breath and breathe out. Now listen and think about the rhythmic model playing within your space. Listen not only from the position of the person sitting at the base of the pyramid, but from the position of the person observing dispassionately and without effort.

From this position try to find similarity between the rhythmic characteristics (tempo, pitch and dynamics) of the model and phenomena of the plant, animal, human world and nature. *This is our goal.* Now slowly open your eyes and look towards the thirteen emotions on the horizontal axis of the matrix. Is there any correspondence between the sound vibrations which you are listening to and the mental elements? Is there anything in the behaviour and attitudes of people, body language and gestures, the flight of birds, swimming of the fish, animals running, the morning dew or tempestuous hurricanes which can be expressed by the sounds you are listening to and which correspond to the emotions in the Virtual Interactive Matrix?

Close your eyes and try to find the correlation between the properties and its mental element, or to be more precise with the vibration which matches the corresponding emotion. Use the associative approach, but on the condition that you use an association beyond the world of your personal perceptions, feelings and mood at the particular moment. The aim of the exercise up to this moment is to take you away from the position of personal perception which may be unclear and wrong, since the world is what we believe it to be, but this does not mean that we are objective.

Separating yourself from the idea of your own ego and your own appreciation of your situation might be the most important and most fragile moment in mental transmutation. If you manage to overcome this barrier you will achieve the possibility of opening the triangular door leading to higher knowledge and enlightenment.

Imagine that "nature" is standing in the place of the person whom you are meditatively observing and that you have to decide on its behalf what the correspondence should be. What would your associations for joy be, for example, and what pictures and sounds would you link to its behaviour? If you cannot at first decide, then repeat the cycle of opening your eyes and look at the matrix (verification) and closing your eyes and listening to the model (correspondence).

When you have found your answer (and there can only be one), take your pencil and note the blank space which corresponds to the emotion which you have chosen.

NOTE: Although the models of step 2 can be practiced at your discretion (depending on the tempos), step 3 must be carried out with one model and strict succession of the four exercises (1, 2, 3, and 4,) without interruption.

The process of effectively defining the mental elements and their characteristic properties can take from a couple of days to months or years. It all depends on how you use the Triangle of Willing Attention and the instructions I have given. Any compromise is not acceptable. The decisions you take and the correspondences you make have to come from outside you, your subjective passions and prejudices. When you have completed all 27 models, we will pass onto the process of analyzing them. It is now time to think about what types of vibrations are emitted by the different types of emotions. Look carefully at the characteristics of the positive, neutral and negative emotions. What are the trends in speed, strength and pitch? Are there any? Your task here is to define how the positive, neutral and negative mental elements vibrate.

> In order to practice the exercises in this chapter, please download the full-length recordings at the following address: www.findhornpress.com/mp3/rhythm.zip

THIRTY-EIGHT

Finding Your Way

*Animals and plants are living effects of Nature; this Nature…
is none other than God in things… Whence all of God
is in all things… Think thus, of the sun in the crocus,
in the narcissus, in the heliotrope, in the rooster, in the lion…
To the extent that one communicates with Nature,
so one ascends to Divinity through Nature.*
— GIORDANO BRUNO

"*This is nonsense!*" a participant in one of my personal development programmes said. The programme involved working with the Virtual Interactive Matrix and expressive media of rhythm and drums. We will have the opportunity to talk about this programme in depth later in this book.

The girl who called out, and others, felt overwhelmed by the decisions and correspondences which needed to be made while working with the matrix to determine their mental characteristics. Part of this difficulty may be that the elements are determined by subjective factors: personal mood, emotional/physical condition, and other factors that surround us. Thus, we can define a rhythm pattern in one way at one time and the next time differently.

It is not easy to abandon the body and mind and make decisions which are not burdened by the weight of your personal convictions. However, this process can be less chaotic when one follows the rules and advice outlined for use of the matrix. One of the main goals of the exercises presented so far is to lead us to a state where we do not think about ourselves and our individual judgments. This is a state in which we remember forgotten knowledge and wisdom.

According to Socrates, humans have nothing more to learn because we already know everything we need. We have simply forgotten it. A true teacher is one who can help us to remember forgotten knowledge. The great Michelangelo perceived his unique creations in rough and uncultured stone blocks. He said that to see the finished sculpture, one only needs to eliminate the unnecessary particles and debris. Like these stone blocks we all possess hidden and forgotten wisdom. To see our true nature we need to separate ourselves from our limited beliefs and understandings. This is the very essence of working with the Virtual Interactive Matrix. If we do not find any meaning, connection or trend in the features and their mental elements, then we are not practicing properly and we are moving in the wrong direction.

Now let me share with you the explanation I gave to the woman I mentioned above. Many of the ills and problems of our social, professional and personal life are associated in one way or another with a violation of the Universal rhythm. Thus one should ask logically, "*What is the correct rhythm and how can we synchronize ourselves with it?*" The answer to this question contains the explanation of the relevance of the Virtual Interactive Matrix. Who or what can show us what is the right and healthy rhythm?

If we are taking part in the performance of the Cosmic Symphony called "*Life*", and we are musicians in that universal orchestra, then each one of us is performing his musical part, trying as hard as possible to be in harmony and balance with the orchestra and the musical landscape. This spectacular composition of "*Life*" has a composer who, depending on our beliefs and convictions, might be a powerful force, energy, God or something else.

To create the complete picture, one more key factor must be presented for the successful implementation of the cosmic symphony. This is the mediator of the composer, namely the conductor. He is the person who knows the entire cosmic score by heart. He is intimately familiar with the variety of tempos, pitches, timbres, dynamics, climaxes and moments of tension and release. If one of us loses our way in the composition, the conductor is there to show him the proper tempo and rhythm.

This conductor is NATURE and we have to conform to its experience and listen to its advice, because it carries the ancient message of the composer. If we turn to NATURE for advice it will be even easier to uncover the correspondences in the matrix. It will be helpful to consider some examples using the photographs on the following page:

RHYTHM ALCHEMY

FIGURE 57

Which of the 13 emotions corresponds to this picture?

Let us now imagine this natural phenomenon: Huge black storm clouds are approaching dangerously, creating an eerie crescendo of sound. The chilling tension explodes in relentless thunder rending the sky and lightning piercing the ground. The roar of the explosion echoes in space and with its low menacing vibrations makes us tremble. I seriously doubt that you have chosen happiness, love, or another one with a positive nuance. I hope that you have found that it is a negative emotion because it has the characteristics of one.

When I give this example everybody without hesitation usually indicates ANGER. You do not even have to imagine the sounds which accompany this natural event to recall the energy it brings – you just know it. However, let us try to determine the characteristics of the rhythm, using the three elements:

> TEMPO – fast
> DYNAMICS – loud
> PITCH – low

Look at the vertical part of the table and find the pattern. If you have not selected ANGER at no. 14, listen to recording no. 28 on the CD included with this book.

Let us leave the stormy scene and go to the deserted beach.

FIGURE 58

Now imagine you are resting on the warm sand with your eyes closed. You breathe in the salty sea air and enjoy the slow, leisurely rhythm of the incoming and retreating waves. Most people name this feeling PEACE. Listen to recording no. 29 and give a definition of its rhythmic parameters:

> TEMPO – slow
> DYNAMICS – soft
> PITCH – medium

As you can see, this emotion which corresponds to pattern #8 from the matrix, is positioned in the neutral / balanced level which brings positive vibrations and sensations.

As a final example I invite you to a forest stream.

Look at the picture and imagine the crystal clear water playfully descending. Fresh water splashes off the rocks onto your face. This image exudes a positive emotion which could be described as JOY.

FIGURE 59

If you are not sure listen to recording no. 30 – lightly flowing water, in order to determine the rhythmic characteristics:

    TEMPO – fast
    DYNAMICS – soft
    PITCH – high

The above characteristics correspond to the pattern no. 1 of the Virtual Interactive Matrix.

These three examples will enable you to tune your perceptions. If your answers match those above, you are moving in the right direction. If even one answer is different, you would benefit from rethinking the reasons for your choice.

Analyze in detail the reasons which brought you to such decisions. Do they come from your ego, opinion, mood, or from the depths of the wise knowledge that is around us? Look to the conductor of the Universal Composition and trust him or her. You can be sure that this is the way.

THIRTY-NINE

Tuning the "strings" – 3rd level

Carefully gather all your thoughts, in order to raise yourself to the beginning of things, to the great trinity which shines in the pure ether.
— ORPHEUS

Some of you perhaps may ask the question, "Why do I need to know all this?" Why do we really need to know what are the rhythmic characteristics of the storm and the stream? Why do we need to know that in the one case the emotion is ANGER and in the other case it is JOY? How can this be of any use to us?

Let me answer this by giving you an example of the strings of musical instruments. Let us begin with a short definition of them: "Strings are vibrating elements which serve as the source of vibrations in string instruments such as violins, guitars, harps and pianos." You have probably seen a guitarist or violinist tune his instrument. One hand tightens or loosens a string while the other checks to see if the desired note has been achieved. The aim of the musician is to tune the string to a specific frequency, in such a way as to vibrate in harmony with the other strings.

In order for this to happen, the musician needs to possess a well-trained musical ear and skill. The example of tuning strings is a wonderful metaphor for what happens when we fine-tune our mental spectrum. The difference is that we are both musicians and musical instruments, whose mental strings and elements are tuned by our knowledge of their properties. The sounds and melodies which fill the ether can be our thoughts, moods, intentions, behaviour and the way in which we speak or move.

If we are tuned harmoniously and give off the corresponding signals, we can then vibrate harmoniously with other people, plants, animals and nature as a whole. If we want to be happy and to possess the ability to affect profoundly other people, to be liked and loved, then we must know the mental range of properties we can use to attune our spiritual strings.

In the previous chapter I gave three examples connected with three mental elements and their properties. In order to achieve proficiency, do not restrict yourself to them, but look for more. Try to find natural phenomena which correspond to the other emotions. When you find them, subject them to a deep analysis. What are their properties (rhythmic characteristics)? You can use all the possible corresponding variations in this entire process.

If we define the natural rhythms as a macrocosm, what then would be the matching corresponding behaviour of the representatives of the microcosm and the entire scale of phenomena in general? For example, how would insects, birds, animals and people express the emotion of HOPE? At first glance the task does not appear easy, but I am certain that you will be able to cope with it. It is just a matter of Will, Attention and Knowledge of emotions!

The knowledge itself will come when you find repetitions and trends in the properties of each level of the scale of phenomena. Your Virtual Interactive Matrix will be full of solutions which will be serious, convincing and indisputable. Then each model, with its corresponding properties of mental elements, will become part of you. You will only have to hear it to define the corresponding emotion. You will only have to refer to the specific emotion in your mind, for one of the twenty seven models to appear in your mind, based on the specific tempo, dynamics and pitch.

From the position of this acquired knowledge and skill, we will pass onto the important step of creating a specific emotional condition. Let us first of all go back to the guitarist and his instrument. He might want to tune the guitar string to "E", and it sounds either higher or lower. Then he has to either loosen or tighten it. Only he can control the correct tone with the vibrations echoing in his conscious mind.

The musician does not think for a moment about how many vibrations the string makes in a second, in order to obtain a note with the correct frequency, he just knows that it is an E. This rule is also completely true for our mental juggling act. However, I need to mention a slight change in the scenario. Instead of trying to tune our flat or sharp string to an E, we will begin with E and we will tune it to a fixed note slightly higher or lower.

In other words, we will determine a neutral/balanced emotional condition and we will create JOY (a higher note) and ANGER (lower note). For this purpose we need to use the properties of the mental elements which we discussed in the previous chapter. For an emotion which expresses neutrality, we won't use PEACE, but NEUTRALITY, which symbolises the "golden mean" with the following logical characteristics:

> Tempo – medium
> Dynamics – moderate
> Pitch – medium

This is the neutral position from which we need either to increase or reduce the vibrations, in order that we can correspondingly create the specific mental condition:

Characteristics	ANGER	NEUTRALITY	JOY
Tempo	fast	medium	fast
Dynamics	loud	moderate	soft
Pitch	low	medium	high

FIGURE 60

Think back to the condition of "timelessness" which we achieved in step 3 of the 2nd level of "Correspondence". This is exactly how you should feel when you are working on tuning your emotional condition. In the process of practising, many people will acquire the skill to immediately enter into the realm of oblivion, while others will need a certain time to prepare. If necessary, repeat the steps from the beginning or do what you think is necessary to swim in the waters of "timelessness".

The basic difference this time is that we will not be using the recording but we will have to imagine it. So when you are both physically and psychologically ready, you will hear a rhythmic pulsation in your mind which has a medium tempo, moderate dynamics and medium pitch. Feel this pulse and let it become part of you. You are now in the neutral position and you do not feel any emotional connection or appetite. Gradually include the verbal sound which bears the characteristics of the model and resonates like a mantra in space. Imagine that this sound is you and that it is pulsating in every cell of your body. When you are completely engulfed by it, then the time has come to change your emotional tuning. This has to happen gradually in the following order:

> *1. Pitch: medium – low*
> *2. Tempo: medium – fast*
> *3. Dynamics: moderate – loud*

To all this add the body movements, gestures and grimaces corresponding to the vibration model. From this condition try to imagine your thoughts going down the road, talking and communicating with strangers, friends and colleagues.

When you become tired, gradually return to the neutral position, changing the rhythmic characteristics in the reverse order and remove the mantra. Now, when you are once again in the condition of "timelessness", just think how you felt when you were attuned to the waves of anger? Can you remember the moments in your life when you acted this way? How did the people who were attracted by the vibrations of your anger react to your destructive emotional vibrations? What were the consequences? How did you feel then? Did you like it? How frequently in your life were such emotional bombs dropped? Do you want them to be a part of it?

When you have answered all these questions, it is time to begin the same tuning procedure, but in the opposite direction by tightening the emotional string. You need to observe absolutely the same instructions and the gradual transition from NEUTRALITY to JOY is accomplished in the following way:

1. Pitch: medium – high
2. Tempo: medium – fast
3. Dynamics: moderate – soft

When you reach joyous vibrations, apply the same techniques which we used in the exercise with anger. Then gradually return to the balanced position. When you have completed the questions and answers which this time are connected to the joyous emotions, take a deep breath, breathe out and open your eyes. Try consciously to pass once again through this vibration adventure in your thoughts. Remember each single detail, sound, gesture and feeling. Compare both emotions and the vibrations characteristic of them. Remember what exactly you did during the emotional tuning. Try to remember the characteristic actions and methods of this tonal transition.

In the same way practice how to tune all the other mental elements. Repeat them, until you can effortlessly pass from the state of NEUTRALITY to each of the other twelve.

At the risk of sounding irritating, I would like to repeat:

The skill lies in doing all this effortlessly!

FORTY

Mental Transmutation – 4th level

*"The art of polarisation" is a stage in "Mental Alchemy",
known and practiced by the ancient and modern hermetic Masters.
To destroy an undesirable rate of mental vibration,
put into operation the Principle of Polarity and concentrate
upon the opposite pole to that which you desire to suppress.
Kill out the undesirable by changing its polarity."*
— THE THREE INITIATES

The Hermetic "Principle of Polarity" is extremely important for this last level of our mental adventure. Let us once again recall what this is:

Everything is Dual; everything has poles; everything has its pair of opposites; like and unlike are the same; opposites are identical in nature, but different in degree; extremes meet; all truths are half-truths; all paradoxes can be reconciled.

Although the principle is defined very accurately and clearly, I believe that it will be very useful to look at it in detail. The most frequent example of the "Principle of Opposites" in Hermetic literature is the example of the thermometer. The thermometer is a device which measures temperature. As a concept, temperature is an entirety which combines a spectrum of higher and lower vibrations which create the feeling of heat or cold. At first glance heat and cold are two extremes but they are in fact two poles of one and the same thing, called temperature.

In the example of the thermometer which expresses temperature, we can see this rule – heat and cold have the same character but they are just different in terms of degree. These concepts are conditional and cannot be absolute because of the same reason. It is very easy for these so-called opposites to pass from one condition to another or to change their places by means of changes in vibrations.

I think that in this case an interesting example is the rhythm which we have been talking about constantly in this book. Rhythm and vibrations are one and the same thing, but they are constructed from opposites – Motion and Rest. Jesus taught us that the sign of God is Motion and Rest. A sign in which Motion effortlessly passes into Rest and back again. This transmutation takes place constantly, to enable vibrations to live as a degree of transformation into other opposites such as Dark and Light, Noise and Silence, Hard and Soft, High and Low, Love and Hate.

When we talk of Love and Hate, we are entering the spectrum of the mental elements in the Virtual Interactive Matrix which we are working with. This is the moment when we have to define our actions connected with the transformation of emotions. For this purpose I would like to offer a suitable extract from Hermetic philosophy:

> Let us take a radical and extreme example – that of "Love and Hate", two mental states apparently totally different. And yet there are degrees of Hate and degrees of Love, and a middle point in which we use the terms "Like or Dislike", which shade into each other so gradually that sometimes we are at a loss to know whether we "like" or "dislike" or "neither". And all are simply degrees of the same thing, as you will see if you will but think a moment.
>
> And, more than this (and considered of more importance by the Hermetists), it is possible to change the vibrations of Hate to the vibrations of Love, in one's own mind, and in the minds of others. Many of you, who read these lines, have had personal experiences of the involuntary rapid transition from Love to Hate, and the reverse, in your own ease and that of others. And you will therefore realize the possibility of this being accomplished by the use of the Will, by means of the Hermetic formulas.

Yes, when I read this extract for the first time, I completely understood the "possibility of doing this", but everything else connected with the transformation was unclear and hazy. I profoundly realized that "Will" is the moving force of this process, but the "Hermetic formulae" which were constantly being referred to and which at the same time remained concealed and veiled in mystery would not give me peace. This was the main reason, to undertake this mental expedition.

Now that we know more about the process, the mental elements, their properties and Hermetic formulae, all these texts acquire a more profound meaning and clarity. From this position now let us look at another extract about another two opposite mental elements of our Virtual Interactive Matrix:

> The transmutation always being between the things of the same kind of different degrees. Take the case of a Fearful man. By raising his mental vibrations along the line of Fear – Courage, he can be filled with the highest degree of Courage and Fearlessness.

We can make a very important conclusion here, ie., that transmutation is possible only between representatives of the same type but with a different degree of vibration. For example, transformation will not be possible between Light and Noisy, Sharp and Soft, Joy and Pride, etc.

The correct and complete understanding of the "Principle of Opposites" contains the key to mastering mental transmutation. The transformation of opposites takes place by sliding along one and the same scale.

For the purposes of greater clarity and practicality, we shall look at two opposing mental elements, which we already know:

PEACE		**ANGER**
Tempo – slow	⟷	Tempo – fast
Dynamics – soft	⟷	Dynamics – loud
Pitch – medium	⟷	Pitch – low

In contrast to the previous level, here the sounds and emotional vibrations will not pass through NEUTRALITY, but will literally slide from one pole to the other. To begin with, for greater ease and to be able to observe how the transformation is achieved, the three characteristics will slide one after another. This is what you need to do:

We start from the position which we already know, "timelessness". At this stage after intensive training at the first levels, you should have achieved the skill of faster and more effective immersion. In this position you will not have any difficulty in generating in your mind the property of the mental element PEACE – pulsations with a slow tempo, soft dynamics and medium pitch. Gradually include a mantra corresponding to these characteristics and let it immerse you completely.

When you decide to undertake mental transmutation, first slide the pitch from medium to low frequency, then the tempo from slow to fast and finally the dynamics from soft to loud. After each of the three steps, take time to synchronize yourself with the new changes in your tuning and then continue until you reach the mental vibration condition of ANGER. When the new emotion immerses you, and you are "enjoying" its destructive force, it is time for us to turn around towards the pole of PEACE. Observe the reverse order of changing the rhythm characteristics – dynamics from loud to soft, tempo from fast to slow and pitch from low to medium.

You can repeat the exercise as many times as you want to and as far as possible do it effortlessly. Practice all the pairs of opposing mental elements, beginning with a positive emotion. I am sure that you will not have problems with grouping the opposites but let me help you:

PRIDE	⟷	**GUILT/SHAME**
JOY	⟷	**SADNESS**
PEACE	⟷	**ANGER**
COURAGE	⟷	**FEAR**
LOVE	⟷	**HATE**

You have clearly seen that two of the mental elements are missing: HAPPINESS and HOPE and their polarities. At first glance these pairs are not apparent, but HAPPINESS is on the scale of SADNESS and JOY, it just vibrates at a higher frequency. The opposite of HAPPINESS is UNHAPPINESS, which is the basic reason for being sad, and fetters us with the chains of SADNESS.

HAPPINESS ⟷ **SADNESS**

When we talk about HOPE, we immediately think of the trinity of FAITH – HOPE – LOVE, where each one of the emotions is part of the other and vice versa. On the other hand HOPELESSNESS and DESPERATION, as the opposite of HOPE, lead to HATE and DETESTATION.

HOPE ⟷ **HATE**

We already have the required opposing mental elements and we will now subject them to the alchemic processes of transmutation which we know.

The aim is through intense practice to achieve the skills of immediate transformation from one condition into another. Gradual sliding and mantras are the instruments we can use, but they gradually have to be removed to leave the pure skill of effortlessly juggling with our emotions.

NOTE: All the exercises discussed up to now can be carried out on a variety of drums and percussion instruments with different pitches and timbres. You do not need to have any musical abilities. The twenty-seven models can be played

with one hand or by two alternating hands. You need to pay special attention to the pitch and timbre of the instrument, which needs to be low, medium or high, depending on the corresponding rhythmic model.

FORTY-ONE

Induction

> *...Atmospheres can be very different – from peace and rest to anger and irritation, from joy to sadness, from anxiety to confidence, etc. They exist around us and move to different places and different people. When someone is in a bad mood, the energy of irritation spreads outside the person and can be felt by someone else at a great distance. One feels and senses the atmosphere of vibrations in the same way as one senses changes in temperature or humidity or the wind.*
> — WILLIAM BLOOM [23]

There are people who assimilate certain skills almost immediately without effort, without stress – almost as if they have been touched by God. For other people the mastery of something new and precious might take huge efforts, nerves, months, years, even an entire life. This is also true of mental transmutation. There is no point in deceiving ourselves but in the process of acquiring the skill, you need to arm yourself with infinite patience, intention, will, desire and energy.

Your achievements will depend on the amount of time and efforts you invest. If you are just interested in the subject, you can just content yourself with reading the book and nothing more. However, if you want to accumulate serious knowledge and then apply it skilfully, then you will need to do more than just read. You need to seek, analyze, apply and practice. According to the ancient Hermetics, the accumulation of knowledge without application and action is tantamount to the pointless and idiotic accumulation of precious metals and stones.

Many of you are probably wondering why I have not presented each mental element in detail with an in-depth analysis, examples, photographs and sounds corresponding to natural phenomena and emotions? Why have I not given more detailed instructions?

---

[23] William Bloom (1948) – British teacher, healer and author in the area of holistic development.

I did this deliberately with the motive of not giving you the opportunity just to accumulate knowledge, but for you to find things out for yourself and use them. My primary task is to make you recall. The fruit and progeny of the alchemic arts must be created by you yourselves. This has to happen by tirelessly subjecting the mental elements and their properties to "heat treatment". In the process of work and by means of accumulated experience with emotions, you need to recreate for yourselves the long lost capstone of ancient knowledge – the Philosopher's Stone.

My book continues from the moment when you have attained that level. You must already possess the categorical skills of effortlessly changing your emotional vibrations allowing you to vibrate at the desired frequencies at all three levels – physical, spiritual and mental. When you are master of your emotions and you are able to provoke and reject them easily, then it is time to begin with induction. Induction is the skill to influence the feelings, thinking and behaviour of other people by means of your emotional vibrations. Let us return to the example of the tuning fork which I gave earlier in the book. We have an unlimited number of tuning forks and each one of them is tuned to 440 hertz.

If we tap one of them and it resonates, all the other tuning forks will begin to resonate at the same note without being touched. This might surprise many people, but this is a normal physical phenomenon and an indisputable fact. Vibrations at 440 hertz cause the other tuning forks to vibrate at the same frequency.

This gives rise to a hypothetical question. If this happens to instruments which are considered to be material objects and devoid of any mental properties and spirituality, then what happens in the case of people? It is very strange that when it affects us, we find it hard to accept phenomena like this. Let me give you another example. If there is no antenna connected to a television and we touch the input connection, we will quickly see a picture begin to form through the "snow". Not only can we receive electromagnetic waves but transmit them as well. Depending on the strength and quality of the emotional signal we emit, we transmit and attract similar vibrations. In this way, and through induction, we can create transformation in the mental condition of other people.

By understanding the type and level of the vibrations of another person, we can direct the opposing mental element of the same type at him or her. For example, if someone is anxious, angry and irritable, we can change his or her emotions by overpowering them with the vibrations of calmness. If we are convinced and insistent of what we are emitting, then the negativism will disappear and the light of change will shine through.

There are many examples of teachers, spiritual enlighteners, revolutionaries, army leaders, political leaders who with the strength of their vibrations influenced not only individuals but entire masses of people and states. Of course, there are both positive and negative examples of this. Although I mentioned earlier in the book that the accumulated knowledge must be used only in a positive direction, it may be that some people may apply it with bad intentions.

I would once again like to emphasize the fact that the negative mental elements in this book are presented, in order for us to learn how not to use them. In order to be happy, you cannot and must not vibrate at the frequencies of SADNESS and ANGER! In order to love and be loved, you cannot and must not vibrate at the frequencies of HATE and FEAR!

It is extremely important to know that by using the emotional element vibrating in our thoughts, we are not only influencing the people but the world around us. There is a significant discovery by Cleve Baxter, an American scientist, which gives proof that plants also have emotions and feelings which are influenced by us. The discovery took place in 1966 when Baxter completely spontaneously decided to attach two polygraph electrodes to a leaf of a plant which he had just watered. He was surprised to see that it reacted in the same way as people who had just experienced a positive emotion.

As a result of this he decided to subject the plant to a destructive test and to observe whether there would be any new emotional changes. The moment he held a burning match to the leaf, the reader of the electrode went mad and began wildly to move across the measurement paper, mapping out the shapes of panic and terror.

This event led to another series of experiments, thanks to which he made some unique discoveries. For example, Cleve Baxter established that plants can react to signals sent to them from a great distance. The apparatus registered positive emotions when he was twenty kilometres away and thought about watering them.

Forty years later the Russian physicist Konstantin Korotkov confirmed the earlier discoveries of Cleve Baxter using more up-to-date equipment. Korotkov attached a mechanism of his own invention called gas discharge visualization to a plant.

This apparatus included a powerful computer, modern optics and digitalized television matrix. The Russian scientist asked his colleagues to think about different feelings such as anger, sadness and joy and then think about specific negative or positive intentions towards the plant. The results showed that the energy field of the plant reduced when it was subjected to a threat and the opposite when a feeling of love was directed at it.

The experiment showed that plants do not just have emotions but can read our thoughts. Why then, if such a primitive living cell is capable of such things, does orthodox science claim that it is impossible for people to read thoughts?

FORTY-TWO

Telepathy

*The wise student hears of the Tao and practices it diligently.
The average student hears of the Tao and gives it thought now
and again. The foolish student hears of the Tao and laughs aloud.
If there were no laughter, the Tao would not be what it is.*

— *LAO TZU*

According to Wikipedia: "*Telepathy (Greek: Τηλ meaning "distant"; and Πάθεια "feeling") is a parapsychological phenomenon in which thoughts and feelings can be transferred between people at a distance without the use of traditional means of technology and equipment. In ordinary words, telepathy can be described as the ability to read thoughts.*"

Since this phenomenon cannot be explained in a "scientific" way, it is believed not to exist. However, as we have already seen from Cleve Baxter's research, the telepathic link between plants and people is completely real. Therefore, the transfer of thoughts and feelings between people should be easier. Is this really the case?

Some years ago I came across an interesting article about telepathy and in which cases it is possible. I shall present a concept which I believe may be the answer to the question.

The figure below shows the normal condition of electrical activity of the brain. Individual A emits vibrations in the form of electrical impulses (thoughts). Gradually the strength of these impulses reduces, since they come up against obstacles of varying types.

When the waves reach the brain of individual B, they are so weak that they are "muffled" by the "noise" of his or her own thoughts. Thus is it impossible for him to assimilate them and read them. It is like being at a reception with lots of people and trying to hear someone whispering at the other end of the room. This example gives a logical explanation of why telepathy is not a frequently encountered phenomenon.

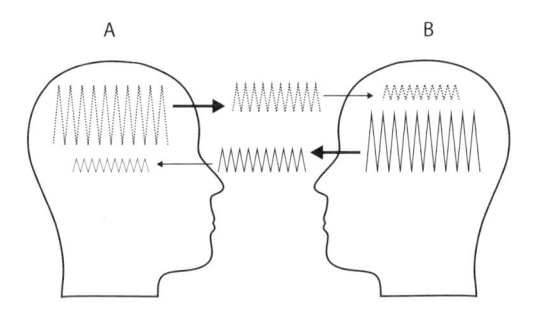

FIGURE 61

The swarms of thoughts which attack our brain and the endless internal dialogue which we have with ourselves completely drown out the thoughts which we receive. By immersing ourselves more deeply in the grey waters of daily problems, it becomes more and more impossible to clear our minds and to open ourselves up to assimilate the information reaching us in a new way. The biggest paradox is that we are living in a time of more rational thought, which actually deprives us of the chance to consider the possibility of telepathy.

Rational thinking just increases the "noise" in our heads. If we want to recognise the emotions and thoughts of people, we will have to stop our internal dialogue and the thoughts buzzing around our own heads. Think back to the different levels in the process of mastering the skills of mental transmutation. These meditational steps were not only intended to be used for the construction of the Virtual Interactive Matrix in your mind, but also to make you cleanse yourselves of unnecessary thoughts and be here and now. Only when silence has overwhelmed your brain, can you feel and hear the thoughts and emotions directed at you.

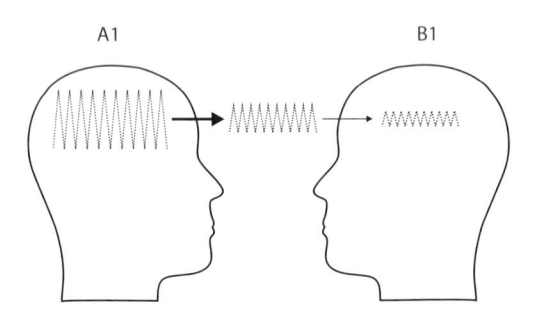

FIGURE 62

In this case individual A1 is in a normal state, while individual B1 has completely mastered the "noise" of his or her thoughts by means of meditation. In this way the electromagnetic waves can be processed and understood – there is nothing in their way to muffle them.

My opinion is that plants capture our thoughts and emotions thanks to this principle. At a primary cellular level they do not need to meditate and to stop their internal dialogue. Plants simply do not have an internal dialogue. Their conscious mind is purified to allow the perception of and reaction to all emotional changes, even if they take place at a great distance.

However, this is not an isolated incident – the same phenomenon can be seen in pet animals. Dogs can perceive their owners from thousands of kilometres away. There have been recorded incidents when the pet owner gets onto a plane in a distant country and the pet is waiting for him the moment he arrives at the front door. Clearly the brain activity of the dog is not great enough to muffle the electromagnetic impulses emitted by its owner.

Let us look at another example in which telepathy is possible, only if the brain waves emitted are stronger than normal. In order for this to happen, they need to be enhanced to such a degree that they drown out the normal brain impulses.

The endless flow of our thoughts can be drowned out only by the destructive emotions of ANGER and FEAR. In this case individual A2 is angry or frightened, and individual B2 is in a normal state and can read the signals being emitted:

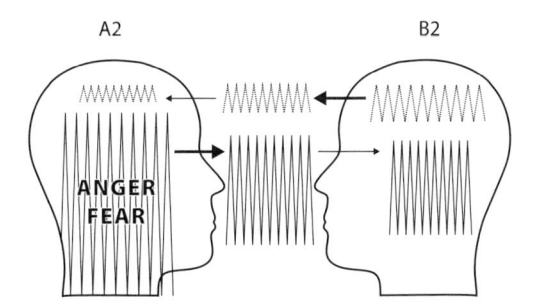

FIGURE 63

Thus in order to read other people's thoughts we need to make them angry or to frighten them. In order to achieve this we need to send the corresponding negative vibrations which will provoke the relevant reaction. This idea clearly does not resonate with the idea of the Unified Rhythm and the general concept of this book. For this reason, I considered whether it might be possible to amplify the vibrations emitted by us in another way?

If this is possible or if there is such an instrument, we would be able to use not anger and fear, but the positive emotions to influence other people.

What would this instrument look like?

PART IV

Ancient Music

FORTY-THREE

Ancient Music

Music is the first expression of the emotions and passions of the heart, it is also the last expression of the emotions and the passions; for what art cannot express, poetry explains; and what poetry cannot express is expressed by music. Therefore to a thinker music in all ages will stand supreme as the highest expression of what is deepest in oneself.
— HAZRAT INAYAT KHAN

I cannot deny that the initial concept I had when I began to write this book, was to structure it in three parts to reflect the idea of trinity throughout the book. I arrived at a moment when the fourth part presented itself to me as an absolute necessity.

I just could not finish the book off so suddenly, the book needed another part. I was concerned that the symbolism and the message of the number 3 would be spoilt, but I had not realized that in this way the structure of my book would be more complete. This fourth part is the final side which encloses the square basis of the pyramid. The trinity when squared (3^2) is equal to 9 – the number which symbolizes the pyramid. In the concept of the micro-macrocosm which I presented here, the Virtual Interactive Matrix is the capstone, and the book is the pyramid.

In this last part of the book I would like to pay more attention to a number of important and useful subjects, which I believe will be a necessary addition and conclusion to the concepts presented here.

I would like to begin with music, but not with the sort of music generally accepted by society. Not the sort of music which we listen to on the radio, in concert halls or in the lobbies and lifts of expensive hotels. I mean *ancient music*. The music which we take for granted and frequently ignore. The melodies, harmonies and rhythms which have always been around and will always be around us.

Music is sound and rhythm. If we could understand the nature and character of rhythm and sound, music would not be used just for entertainment, but would be a source for survival. Listen to the sound of the falling leaves, the sound of raindrops gradually growing louder on your window sill, the flashes of lightning in the sky and the rumbling of thunder signifying the onset of autumn rain.

Imagine the dancing snowflakes, the fir trees heavy with snow, the frozen streams and listen to the voice of the winter storm and the rhythmic drops of thawing icicles. Listen to the blossoming of the trees, the quiet and playful trickling of the river, the buzzing of the insects, the hooves of the deer and the rhythmic tapping of the woodpecker, announcing the awakening of nature. Feel the sea breeze, the scent of the sea, the splashing of the diving fish, the rhythmic roaring of the waves and the calls of the seagulls circling above the water.

Without doubt this is the music which resonated from the magic lyre of Orpheus and took the breath away from every living being. Music which has nothing in common with our artistic tastes, but with its vibrations, contains the ability to transform. Let us think about this question. It has been proven that neither the ancient lyre of Orpheus, nor the musical language of that time possessed rich expressional qualities. In fact the functionality of the lyre was quite limited. Orpheus' lyre was recently recreated on the basis of ancient drawings and information.

The project was funded by the European Project "Musicabili" (Ancient musical instruments). Milena Valcheva, the musician who had the honour of playing the instrument and wrote special music for it, wrote:

> ..."The capabilities of the instrument are very limited, only seven notes can be played on it. It has not been an easy task to create a melody from these seven tones which might sound sufficiently artistic."

How then did Orpheus achieve his magic? Clearly he achieved this by his skill of mental transmutation, and his alchemic musical instrument channelled his enormous spiritual energy. As I mentioned earlier, the nature of this lyre possesses seven hermetic principles which are manifested under the influence of the magical sounds of Orpheus. Geraldine Pinch, the famous Egyptologist, believes that:

> In Hermeticism, as well as in the Jewish and later Judean Kabbala, sounds, words and even individual letters can represent the equivalent of charge cells, reservoirs of energy, filled with a special form of divine or magic energy, just like a battery charged with electrical energy.

One such reservoir of divine energy in which the enlightened Orpheus was charged with knowledge and spiritual potential was the Great Pyramid. By charging himself with Hermetic "electricity", he transformed himself into a similar high-energy reservoir capable of charging people with positive vibrations. His lyre not only gave life to the magical healing sounds, but also amplified his divine thoughts and intents.

In fact it is no wonder that every living thing fell silent and listened to him in wonderment. Orpheus, the master of alchemic art, achieved mental transformation which muffled the noise of thoughts and the internal dialogue, but not via the destructive influence of anger and fear. His lyre amplified the life-giving healing emotions and the feelings of love, joy and happiness. One of Orpheus's most famous verses which has survived to our days is: *The earth can be conquered with a lyre, not by the sword!*

FORTY-FOUR

The Ancient Alchemical Instrument

Drumming with a purpose is the difference between a light bulb and a laser beam. When people come together to drum, be it in a ritual form, such as a solstice gathering for the changing of the seasons or trance drumming to travel where the mind becomes quiet, or Shamanic drumming where physical healing takes place, then you use the drum as a laser beam rather than a light bulb.
— ARTHUR HILL [24]

I can honestly say that despite my serious professional education and commitment to the world of music, I played the drums meaninglessly for 25 years. I did not realize that I held in my hands the most ancient alchemic instrument, older than Orpheus' lyre. Gifted with the selfish motives typical for every performing artist, I illuminated myself and the people around me with the weak light of the electric light bulb. The miracle happened when I forgot about myself and began to play meaningfully.

In this process, it is not you playing, but the music playing through you, like light refracting through a crystal. Every time I touched the instrument with desire and the intention of making a positive effect, the atmosphere around me filled with a magical energy which removed all inhibitions and psychological barriers. Talking with the universal language of rhythm, I began to penetrate deeper and deeper into the intimate cells of human consciousness and to model positive moods and emotions.

I realized that this ancient instrument possesses strength greater and is more significant than Orpheus's lyre. The drum has the power to be a more powerful amplifier of positive and healing vibrations than string instruments such as the lyre. Its sounds have the ability to penetrate more deeply into the depth of our

---

[24] Arthur Hill – World famous facilitator of public and social rhythm events. One of the founders of the Drum Circle movement at the end of the 20th century.

perceptions and more successfully to synchronize with our vibrations. Moreover, taking into account its nature and the fact that rhythm is a part of all of us, it is easy to use and can become an alchemic instrument in the hands of anyone. We do not need to have musical abilities and special training to create a composition of emotions with percussion instruments.

In the hands of even the most inexperienced performer the drum can whisper like the waves of the sea, can trickle like a forest stream, vibrate in time with the thunder claps of a destructive storm. This instrument has richer and more flexible capabilities to express the ancient music – music which affects and heals. The drum can work upon negative moods, emotions and feelings, by allowing us to free ourselves of them and recharge us with new, fresh vibrations. The drum helps us to participate actively in the process of mental transformation and attain the secret skills of the Thracian musician.

With the decoded Hermetic formulae of mental transmutation and the alchemic instrument which helps amplify our intentions and transform negative emotions, I discovered infinite new possibilities, and I was capable of changing reality. I began to organize and conduct a wide range of public, social, educational, corporate, therapeutic and healing activities based on rhythm and the expressive resources of drums and percussion instruments.

Over the past ten years I have managed to hold a large number of educational courses, workshops and seminars, motivational and corporate training sessions, teambuilding[25] events, therapeutic sessions and other events. Participants have included people from a wide range of social status, age, education, ethnicity and health conditions.

Despite the above-mentioned variety of participants and the initial state of their spirit when beginning the sessions, they all had one resembling feature – the smiles on their faces at the end of the sessions. Even the biggest sceptics turned into the most active participants under the influence of the energy of the drums. During these rhythm holidays not only was I able to play the drums meaningfully, but also entire groups of people had come in and made contact with the instruments for the first time. I was delighted to have the chance to bring the "music" of other people out into the open, rather than my music.

I realized that I was able to help them compose and perform with the feelings, emotions of their unique internal voices, without possessing special qualities, musical talent and without speaking even a single word. Then their music becomes my music, and this becomes our music – into world art.

---

25 Teambuilding – This term refers to the development and collective motivation of corporate units.

The art of our past, present and future. The art of our existence. All this is thanks to the drum – an instrument as ancient as humanity itself.

FORTY-FIVE

Restrictive Beliefs and Convictions

If, then, thou hast the power, He will, Tat, manifest to thy mind's eyes. The Lord begrudgeth not Himself to anything, but manifests Himself through the whole world. Thou hast the power of taking thought, of seeing it and grasping it in thy own "hands", and gazing face to face upon God's Image. But if what is within thee even is unmanifest to thee, how, then, shall He Himself who is within thy self be manifest for thee by means of [outer] eyes? But if thou wouldst "see" him, bethink thee of the sun, bethink thee of moon's course, bethink thee of the order of the stars. Who is the One who watcheth o'er that order?

— HERMES TRISMEGISTUS

"*I have no sense of rhythm*", "*I have no talent, or attitude to rhythm/music and I am not sure that I could take part in rhythm sessions*", "*I'll make a fool of myself in front of the others*".

These are the most frequently encountered doubts and programmed inhibitions, which I hear from potential participants in the various events and programmes linked to the various forms of rhythm therapy I offer. I could actually admit that most of the programmes which I created are dedicated to people who consider that they have no sense of rhythm.

Where do these doubts and erroneous convictions about our abilities come from? They usually originate at an early age when some "*competent authority*" points a finger at us and tells us, "*You have no sense of rhythm*". This conviction begins to live within us, to feed from us and what is worst of all – it becomes part of us. There is nothing left for us than to believe that we have no sense of rhythm and tremble in fear when we are faced with the challenge. All this sounds completely paradoxical, since if we had no sense of rhythm, our bodies would just fall apart.

The billions of cells from which we are constructed, work together in a synchronous rhythm to form the basis of the vital processes. "*Have I got a sense of rhythm?*"

For me this is like asking: "*Can I breathe?*", "*Can I talk?*", "*Can I walk?*", "*Can I live?*" Many people probably do not realize that rhythm is genetically programmed in our system as a direct result of how we appear in this world. During the nine months spent in our mother's womb, every individual accepts and encodes the rhythm of her heart within their own organism. This is the same rhythm, which under the pressure of the erroneous convictions within us, we see as alien, unfamiliar, strange and even extravagant. This leads to the fear of the unknown and of mistakes: "*What will people say if I make a mistake, and if they realize that I don't have a sense of rhythm?*"

Let us return to our early childhood years and recall how we were spoon fed. "*This spoonful is for mummy. This spoonful is for daddy. This is for your brother… and if you don't eat it all up, the monster will come and get you!*" With this fear instilled in us, we crossed the threshold of our first nursery class, primary school, high school and university, where we were taught restrictively, and pedantically, by people who were also afraid of the Monster, but at a different level.

They taught us that it is wrong and fatal to make mistakes. So how can we develop if we do not make mistakes or accumulate the experience we need for life? Woody Allen, the famous American film director said:

> If we don't make mistakes, it means we're not trying.

These fears and hesitations seem to conceal the problems of our time. In the dynamics and confusion of modern life we frequently forget some very simple and evident truths. It seems to have become "fashionable" for hyperactive brain activity to lead us into endless labyrinths of thoughts about whether we are valuable, valid, financial and socially competitive in this confused and messed-up world.

At the fast rate of the life we are living, we do not pick up the impulses and signals which are sent to us by the source of our real nature, life, purity and love. Our hearts seem less and less to take part in our "thought processes", spontaneous actions and decision-taking. The metronome which measures the tempo of our life has long ago been lost under the cobwebs of our rational minds.

In the same way that Michelangelo removed the unnecessary parts of the rough stone blocks, in order to reveal the beauty of his immortal creations, in the same way we need to divest ourselves of our restrictive beliefs and convictions, in order to reveal our real essence.

I have seen this process take time and effort, but at the same time I have also witnessed how vibrations of the drum dispel these fears and inhibitions in minutes. During group drum playing, a unique process can be observed. Borne aloft on the wings of rhythm, we are on the one hand carried into the realm of vibrations, while on the other hand remaining in the here and now.

Although we use our motor movements to create a rich sound palette in space with a wide range of dynamics and amplitude, we are also witnesses to our silent mind and silent brain. The internal dialogues cease, we have immersed our ego in the present moment and without realizing it, we perceive the pure vibrations of other people. Our conscious mind is open to accepting the unique nature of each other person in the group and our reactions are a sign of accepting actual reality. Fear and doubts disappear, since no one is testing us, pointing at us or condemning us.

We are participating in a creative process, using our unique internal voices which create an inimitable sound picture. These are magic moments in which the participants are purified under the influence of vibrations.

Almost always, after such an event, the greatest sceptics and those who actively refuse to participate in the rhythm adventure do not want to leave. They sit there excited and filled with the desire for another portion of vibrating elixir.

They are no longer afraid and not hesitant. They just want to continue.

FORTY-SIX

Rhythm Session in Prison

We have to find a way to make our hearts feel safe and secure in order to renew and nurture the love that lived there as a child, the love that will help us find a rhythm and a power to our lives that will serve us instead of hinder us.
— *JIM GREINER*[26]

It is difficult for "normal law-abiding" members of society to define what it is to be behind bars, or how prisoners feel and what they need. We do not use the word "prisoner" and we pretend not to have heard it, or that it does not exist. Sooner or later, whatever crimes they may have committed, these people will once again come back into our society, and whether or not they will break the law again depends not only on them, but all of us. Our attitude, thinking and actions have to focus on greater tolerance, care and sensitivity.

The Rhythm Therapy session which I held in the Sofia Central Prison as part of the "Movable Bars" project was aimed at building a creative and safe environment for each participant to create their own moods, thoughts, emotions and remove psychological barriers and blocks. One of my primary aims was not only to lay the foundations of a new form of therapy, which might successfully be applied in prisons around the world, but to show the need for them.

The rhythm session was welcomed by the prisoners with euphoria and was a great success. The participants were seated in circles and each was given a drum or percussion instrument which they would use to express their emotional state and uniqueness. Gradually each one of them was drawn into a common rhythm and the varied palette eloquently drew a picture in sound. There was not a trace of the severe and cautious expressions which had met us in the beginning.

They had melted away and now their eyes glistened with joy, while their broad

---

26 Jim Greiner – Internationally recognized percussionist, teacher, rhythm facilitator and inspiring orator.

FIGURE 64
Rhythm emotions in the Sofia Central Prison

smiles brightened the severe and gloomy atmosphere. Those for whom there was no room in the circle danced and uttered sounds of joy, breathing with the common rhythm and adorning it with additional ornamentation. The participants reached a point of common catharsis which made the moment unforgettable for all those present.

Despite the entertaining form of the session, the participants realized at a conscious and subconscious level that they were part of something serious. Each one of them had a specific function in the common rhythm and without his conscious participation and help the result would not have been the same. Each of them was able to share their own uniqueness in the way they wanted without being criticised, sworn at or pointed at. They all realized that with their own uniqueness they were contributing at that one moment to the collective rhythm landscape.

The hostility, arguments, problems and conflicts between them no longer existed. Each one felt more responsible and concerned that the result would be successful for all of them. They openly expressed their desire to help the others who might not have understood something correctly. They were no longer rejected, unnecessary and superfluous members of this society, but serious artists creating a composition in which they were the musical scores and their emotions and feelings, the musical notes. The group energy had reached its culmination and we had all forgotten where we were.

The inner dialogue, inhibitions and problems had disappeared and the group was in the realm of rhythm where everyone was equal, unique, creative, important and more important. Even concealed aggression was expressed in a more delicate, less insulting and less injurious way.

The Drum/Rhythm Therapy session ended, as it began, with congratulations and handshakes. This time when I shook everyone's hands I could feel that their grip was not as rough and severe, and that their eyes were filled with gratitude. Many of them asked me, *"When will we see you again?"* I did not know what to answer. I felt sad that I could not promise anything to people who clearly had a daily need for something like this. I felt guilty that it was not up to me, and that I could not give them the answer they wanted. Then I realized that at this stage there was only one response I could give to everyone who asked the question:

"Do our prisons need Rhythm Therapy?" and the answer is *"Yes, absolutely!"*

FORTY-SEVEN

Corporate Rhythm

> *An inspiring experience! How else could you describe in words this feeling of spiritual "teleportation" from the stressful daily life into the world of art and the rhythm of the drums. A team-building experience in which my colleagues and I were not just participants but creators recreating through sound and rhythm the emotion that we are all ONE.*
> — *B.M.*, Senior Vice-President of an international Energy company

When I first presented my idea for corporate drum training sessions, many of the human resources managers I met treated me sceptically. Many of them found it difficult to imagine how the use of percussion instruments could make any difference to serious and responsible company matters.

The problem here was the word "drum" was being used out of context. The key word is "rhythm" and the drum is not just a means of entertainment but a channel for the wide range of vibrations and rhythmic forms. As we have already seen in this book, rhythm forms the basis of our existence and the main factor which directs it. The drum is more like a painter's brush – we use it to depict the picture of our rhythm by means of the diverse palette of emotions, moods and behaviour.

In the world in which we live there are many diverse groups of people united around a common idea – these are called collectives. The most common collectives are sporting teams, creative groups and commercial companies. In the most general terms, what is true of business collectives, can also be said of creative and sporting collectives. Everyone works and makes efforts aimed at creating a given product – the team plays to win a trophy; the orchestra plays together to perform a symphony; the working collective works together to produce and sell a product or service.

The qualities and values which contribute to a successful musical event are similar to those in the working process. They include: cooperation, active listening, flexibility, respect for individual differences, mutual assistance and effective communication. I have gradually managed to convince companies of the importance of such a programme and thus "Corporate Rhythm" was born. (This is a professional programme which incorporates rhythm in the training of diverse types of corporations.)

"Corporate Rhythm" offers mental challenges associated with the composition and arrangement of musical elements which in turn leads to enhancing the individual abilities of logical thinking, decision-taking and problem-solving. Since music is a non-verbal form of communication, it allows people to share ideas and concepts which go further than the confines of language, culture and tradition.

Over the past five years world famous energy, telecommunications, IT, motor, finance and banking companies have experienced the "Corporate Rhythm" programme and offered useful soft skills[27] training to their collectives. These skills include:

- Stress management
- Conflict solving
- Time management
- Leadership
- Building support and trust
- Inter-personal communication, active listening and feedback
- Integration, synchronicity and balance
- Balance between work and a personal life
- Personal and group motivation.

In a large number of training and team-building events the participants were able to look at themselves or their colleagues from a perspective different to that of their daily working environment. Their active involvement in specially prepared rhythmic metaphors allowed them to draw a parallel between their experience and their specific working environment.

In this way they learnt through experience and were able to draw their own useful conclusions. They were also able to see that playing the drums with their colleagues is a good way of having fun and learning that working together in synchronicity is not unattainable.

---

27 Soft skills – Sociological term relating to personal coefficients of emotional intelligence. A collection of personal characteristics, social elegance, communication, language, personal habits, friendship and optimism which characterize relations with other people.

I could recount some quite interesting and inspiring cases in which the participants achieved individual and group catharsis. Events filled with moving emotions, laughter and tears. I would like to tell you an unforgettable story which happened with the team of a large company from the energy sector.

It was a group of about thirty people and the training session was going very well. This was helped by the good energy of the collective and their desire to take an active part in the rhythm activities which I had presented to them. We were about to do one of my favourite exercises. We were sat in a large circle and everyone was at a comfortable distance from their colleagues, to the right and left. The participants' arms were stretched out in front of them, and each was holding in their left hand a coloured shaker [28] egg.

The aim was to pass the eggs from left to right and in a very strict tempo take the egg from the left hand with the free right hand and place it in the left hand of the colleague to the right. All this was to take place in absolute synchronicity and the sound made by the passing of the instruments was to be like the sound of a single person. This exercise is very useful, not only because it very clearly symbolizes the idea of working in synchronicity, but also shows that a chain is only as strong as its weakest link. This is exactly what happened.

I normally begin this exercise at a slow tempo and dynamics and gradually increase them as the participants get accustomed to it. The problem I noticed was happening even at slow speed. We were unable to pass the eggs on in synchronicity because the chain always broke in a certain place. I looked in that direction and saw the person who was the "weak link". I approached him with the desire of giving him further explanations, but I realized that something was not quite right.

I have a principle of shaking every participant's hand before the event. This is my way of shortening the distance between us and making things more personal. I recalled that when I had shook this man's hand in the beginning I felt something strange, but had not paid much attention to it. Up to that moment I had not noticed a particular problem with him, but when I looked carefully I was shocked. The middle-aged man had no fingers on his right hand, just a palm. He could not grab the egg or pass it on. This was the real problem.

I was upset not because he had no fingers, but because I had not noticed it at the beginning of the session. If I had known, I would probably not have used the exercise. After all, my role as facilitator was to make the process easier, not to make it harder. Given these circumstances we were clearly unable to perform the task and

---

28 Shakers – Percussion instruments consisting of a variety of hollow bodies of different types of material filled with sand, seeds, rice or beans. They are played by shaking them.

I had to take the right decision very quickly. All the possible options and alternatives spun past my eyes like a film strip, but I could not find a fast solution.

The situation was becoming more tense and irreversible when salvation came from the man with no fingers. He made a very simple movement which changed everything and gave even more meaning to the entire exercise. He turned around to stand with his back to the centre of the circle and put the egg on the palm of his hand with no fingers.

In this way his colleague could put the percussion instrument on his palm, and he could pick it up with his left hand and pass it along the chain.

FIGURE 65
The man (to the right) who became the leader of the group

The movement in the whole group was from left to right, except for him – where it was from right to left. Despite this everything took place with absolute finesse and synchronicity. The outsider of the group had become its leader and he was using his disadvantage to create a unified and solid rhythm. The expression on everyone's face showed not pity but trust and respect. They all realized that they were taking part in a magical moment of personal and collective transformation. The next day they would all be looking at themselves, their colleague and the entire collective in another way.

"The weakest link" would prove the strength of the entire chain!

FORTY-EIGHT

Rhythm and Autism

They have a sensitivity to sound and poor social interaction skills. I feel the most important thing in working with autistic kids is to meet them where they are. In their world, they are totally alone.
— DR. BARRY BERNSTEIN [29]

Over recent years I have presented the use of rhythm therapy for autism in many towns in the country. A large number of specialists in this country, parents and autistic children were able to see the transforming power of rhythm. During two successive sessions I show first adults, then the children and their parents, a number of techniques connected with the therapy.

These events are usually reported on the national and regional media and the most frequent question I am asked is: "*What positive effect does rhythm have on autistic children?*" In order to answer this question, first of all I have to explain what autism is. It is important to understand that this is not an illness, but rather a state of mind. Since everything around us is vibrations, our bodies, organs and thoughts also vibrate at a given frequency.

Autistic children vibrate at a frequency different to that of other people. This creates a different state of mind leading to a behaviour which is less acceptable for society. It is important to note that living in this different state of vibrations, they can attain and process special information which unlocks incredible abilities.

In recent years horse therapy, (hippo-therapy) and dolphin therapy have become popular. You might wonder how these animals might be useful, but they really are able to perceive the world of autistic children and attune themselves to their frequency. However, they are unable to bring the children out of this state

---

29 Barry Bernstein (1954 – 2009) – Musical therapist who developed a variety of programmes and activities based on rhythm and drums. He is well-known for his work with war veterans and his avant-garde scientific research with dementia patients.

and bring them closer to the more acceptable standards of behaviour. *This can be achieved with rhythm.*

In the form of having fun with percussion instruments we can attune ourselves to the level of vibrations of autistic children and meet them in a safe place – in their territory. Then we can gradually draw them out of their world and by means of rhythm we can work in the direction of positive changes.

Many of us cannot imagine what this altered state of mind is really like and how autistic children vibrate in a different way. For this reason I always begin my presentation with an example which demonstrates the process. This exercise is quite similar to the exercises connected with mental transmutation shown in this book, except that we use drums.

All the participants are arranged in a circle and each one of them has an instrument. I make a short presentation about drums and various other percussion instruments. I explain the non-verbal communication signs and invite the participants to close their eyes. Then I ask them to try and observe themselves. How do they feel at the moment? What is their physical and psychological condition? Are they feeling any pain? If yes, what exactly? Do they have any specific emotions? Are they afraid of anything? Are they worried? What is their state of mind?

I need a few minutes for this preparatory part of the session, after which I take them through a vibration alchemy process, in which I literally bombard them with cascades of rhythmic emotions. We all play and improvise together while I synchronize the groups in constantly altering tempos, timbres and dynamics.

In actual fact what I offer them is a rhythm cocktail of mental elements and their properties with the basic aim of transforming the momentary mental states of the participants. Within the space of 15 minutes, dozens of rhythmic metamorphoses take place, ending with the development of a fast and steady rhythm.

When the room falls back into silence, I invite them to close their eyes again and to state their psychological and physical condition. Then I ask them:

> "Open your eyes and remember how you felt before the session. Is there anyone in the room who believes that no change has taken place in their conscious mind?"

No one has ever raised their hand to say that nothing has changed or that their emotions have remained unchanged. This is an exceptionally useful exercise, because the participants can consciously register the changes in the scale of their mental world and see that by the end of the process they are different. When they leave the room and meet other people who have not taken part in the rhythm circle, they definitely feel different from them.

In the same way, this difference becomes manifest in autistic children. They are enclosed within their own vibration world and very frequently their behaviour goes beyond the framework of familiar stereotypes.

At such moments two of the greatest problems of autism are most noticeable. Autistic children are unable to focus their attention on one specific thing for any length of time, and they have a problem communicating with others. I would like to tell you a story which happened during one of the therapy demonstrations.

I noticed him as I was bringing the drums into the room where the session was going to be held. There was a little boy running on his tiptoes up and down the long corridors of the buildings, shrieking and making all sorts of noise. He would occasionally stop and gesticulate with his arms. This seemed to provide him with the auto-stimulation he needed. He looked about 10 years old and I tried to talk to him. I saw that he could not talk and that he had difficulties communicating.

His parents were following him but they also appeared to have problems restraining and coping with him. They later told me that he communicated with no one and that it was almost impossible to focus his attention on anything for more than a few seconds. They also apologized to me in advance that they probably would not be able to remain in the drum circle, since Danny would not be able to focus for more than a minute.

I told them not to worry and started preparing for the rhythm session. When all the children gathered with their parents, I arranged them in a circle and gave them a drum each.

The smaller children sat with their parents while the older children had their own chairs. There was one empty seat and someone was obviously missing. I looked around and saw that my friend, Danny, was missing. I then saw his father dragging him by the hand, and he was pulling away. I waited for them to sit down. Danny sat on his father's knee and there was a huge drum in front of them. It seemed as though the little boy was not going to be able to sit still for very long, but things changed radically.

This happened when I began to show different exercises with one hand and then with the other, and the children had to follow me. We touched the drums and made rhythmic sounds while I counted from one to four. Danny, who until a few moments before had been running tirelessly up and down the corridors, shrieking at the top of his voice, was now sitting in stunned silence! He was drinking in the information which he was receiving. His father was helping him play the drum and he occasionally took a turn with louder or softer sounds.

FIGURE 66
My friend Danny

In this way Danny was communicating with the entire group and having fun at the same time. The father and son remained in the circle to the very end of the rhythm session, which lasted for almost half an hour. His father could not believe what had just happened in front of his very eyes. He could not recognize his son in this light – he was calm, focused and communicative.

The most important thing in this process, in which the father was helping him to play and take part in the group, was that they created a relationship which until that moment had been impossible. Rhythm was that bridge which had crossed the gap between them. Danny's father had tears of joy and excitement in his eyes.

A few weeks later, Danny began to come to me for individual rhythm therapy sessions. As soon as I opened the door, he smiled and came in. His parents told me that he did not like going anywhere, especially to strange places.

Rhythm had clearly done its job and Danny had grown to like me.

I have always wondered why dolphins and horses have been able to achieve this special link with autistic children, while we "normal" people have difficulties.

FORTY-NINE

The Old Man and the Drums

*While we have the gift of life, it seems to me the
only tragedy is to allow part of us to die – whether it is
our spirit, our creativity or our glorious uniqueness.*
— *GILDA RANDER*[30]

On the 22nd March, in synchronicity with the advent of spring, I received an email which acted like a breath of fresh air to arouse my drowsy winter sensations. The letter was sent to me by the Director of the "Ilio Voivoda" Home for Adults with Physical Disabilities in Kustendil, Bulgaria. She kindly and joyously was inviting me to visit them and entertain the residents of the home with my rhythm. I was also excited because I was born in Kustendil and I had never presented my rhythm therapy there. It was a wonderful opportunity to meet specialists from that city and undertake therapy with adults who needed attention and care.

Since it was just before Easter, I decided that this would be my Easter present for them. It was Easter Friday and I had arranged the circle of chairs, drums and percussion instruments and waited for the first part of the programme to start – a presentation of the therapeutic force of rhythm to the specialists. At all presentations like this I try to retell the content of this book in a few simple sentences and to add a few scientific facts, if anyone shows interest.

I am used to the scepticism of some of the participants at events like this. This presentation was no exception, but I was not in the least worried, because I knew that after this I would be giving a live demonstration. Then the waterfall of sounds and rhythm flowed over every one of the participants and the alchemic process was beginning.

About thirty-five psychologists, psychotherapists, social workers and pedagogues were playing the percussion instruments like a single person, even though

---

30 Gilda Radner (1946 – 1989) – Famous American comic actress.

they did not know each other, they had not rehearsed together and had not even touched a musical instrument. At my sign they all categorically emphasized the final beat of the performance on their instrument and immediately the vibrations of what had just taken place resonated in the form of amazed exclamations, happy laughter and loud applause.

At that moment all my words are meaningless, because only through live experience, you can understand exactly what is taking place during such a rhythm session. There was not a trace of the previous mistrusting looks and we were friends, congratulating each other, laughing and discussing future projects.

I came back to reality when through the open door of the room I saw a group of adults in wheelchairs looking in and showing unconcealed curiosity and impatience. At that moment I recalled the real reason for my visit – a rhythm session for the disabled adults. About fifteen minutes later, the room was full of people sitting in wheelchairs. I introduced myself to each one of them personally and was able to get an impression of their condition.

There were people in the room with total or partial paralysis, loss of limbs, multiple sclerosis, blindness and Alzheimer's. The age range was between 65 and 85, and two Roma women, aged around 35, had mental disabilities. A very important element of this type of therapeutic session is the correct choice of percussion instruments. The choice has to take into account the limited physical abilities of the participants. Some were given drums which they could play with one or both hands, others were given maracas [31] of varying sizes, and two women who could not move, listened. They were wonderfully innocent and kind people.

They were holding something in their hands and had no idea how to use it, but they clearly wanted to. I could see that unlike the previous group, they had no burdening thoughts or doubts. They just wanted to be part of something which would make their life more bearable and bring a little bit of joy. They wanted to have fun and were sitting like children in front of the window of a sweet shop waiting to be invited in.

I gave them simple instructions about how to use the instruments and explained the non-verbal signs which I would use to enable them to follow me. I played a Latino-American rhythm on my CD player and I gradually began to synchronize the group to it. Very soon "Spring" came for the people in the home. Smiles blossomed on their faces, and their eyes were filled with real joy. This was something new for them, but at the same time something which they had always known.

---

31 Maracas – Type of shaker from Latin America.

I watched while the rhythm seemed to transform them and make them younger. The dynamics in the groups increased and many of them were playing beyond the level of their motor abilities. There were no rules; they just had to follow the rhythm, while I cut off slices of the musical cake for them. The two Roma women were the two most faithful assistants filling the group with energetic emotional portions of rhythm and laughter.

Suddenly the door opened and another participant in a wheelchair arrived late. I moved the man into the circle and invited him to play. He categorically refused but five minutes later I saw him pull his neighbour's drum towards him. The only standing participant was a dear little grandmother who was leaning clumsily against the wall holding a big maraca in her right hand. The rhythmic movement she was performing came from her wrist, while her left hand shook. There were tears in her eyes, but she continued to play and to be part of the big magic. In the frame of the open door stood the staff of the home.

They were all swaying their heads in rhythm and could not believe the transformation taking place with their patients.

FIGURE 67
Unforgettable therapeutic rhythm session in the Ilio Voivoda Home for Adults with Physical Disabilities, Kustendil.

One of the two women who were not performing was sitting silently with a percussion egg in her lap. Her face was cold and expressionless and she looked at me as though I did not exist. There was no emotion in her face, even though we were all in the rapture of this rhythm fiesta. During the entire time I tried to observe her and to attract her attention, but without success.

Even though everyone was happy and the atmosphere was incredible, I began to feel a sense of defeat until something unforgettable and astounding happened. We were approaching the end of the rhythm session when the woman slowly lowered her head and looked at the percussion egg in her lap. Then she slowly and gradually returned her head to the horizontal position and looked me in the eyes.

I was kneeling in front of her, smiling and playing the big drum. This time she looked at me with awareness. She could see me. A short, barely perceptible, smile brightened up her face and remained there for about five seconds, after which she descended back into her previous state and could no longer see me. I was later to discover that she had Alzheimer's syndrome and I was exceedingly happy that I had managed, even for a second, to arouse a memory of emotions in her.

Our concert was heading towards its end and the participants were performing to their utmost and with complete commitment. The finale came after an avalanche-like tremolo performed by the entire group.

Their spontaneous and immediate applause sounded like part of the performance itself. It was filled with gratitude, recognition and respect for themselves and the others – they were both the performers and the public. It was a real pleasure to watch these smiling and inspired adults. They were filled with energy and cheer. They began to leave the room with smiles on their faces, thanking me as they left.

An old man who had been one of the most active drummers slowly approached me in his wheelchair. He took my hand, kissed it and through his tears he said: "*Thank you, son!*"

I could hardly keep my own tears back and I leant down and kissed his hand. As I did it, I thought that it was worth living for what had just happened .

This was my present for the holidays! Thank you!

FIFTY

The Children from Doganovo

We are born with a need for rhythmic input. It affects how our brain waves function and may play an important role in normal physical, emotional and intellectual development.
— DR. KAY ROSCAM, Director of the department of music therapy of Chapman University, CA, USA

It has been established that children laugh about three hundred times a day, and adults only fifteen. Although this may be explained by the fact that adults are burdened with the serious problems of life, the real conflict lies elsewhere. It is a problem, however, when there are children who smile and laugh less than fifteen times every day, and their number in Bulgaria is not insignificant.

The huge number of children deprived of parental care, and hospitals for disabled children, are filled with sad faces longing for smiles and attention.

How can we help them? How can we be useful? What can we do to make these children smile and help them with the advice and knowledge they need for the life which lies before them?

The "Smile and Make Someone Happy!" initiative which the LIBERA Institute for Contemporary Art and Therapy developed more than a year ago, contains the response to all these questions. As a non-governmental organisation aimed at benefiting society, our intention was focused on the idea of uniting the business and the non-governmental sector to help provide benefits for children with illnesses and also children deprived of parental care.

Our main aim was to create opportunities, events and initiatives with the aim of enhancing the emotional and physical health of children from the above-mentioned groups, by means of rhythm and percussion instruments.

20km from Sofia, close to Elin Pelin, is the village of Doganovo. In the village school building there is a home for children deprived of parental care. Just over one year ago I met the 50 wonderful children who live in this home. Our relationship and friendship has grown very strong and this is all thanks to rhythm. In 2010 we began with a single rhythm therapy session as part of the "Smile and Make Someone Happy!" initiative. The sounds, rhythm, drums and other percussion instruments took the children to a new world of feelings and a means of expression and communication.

Over the next year we created a special project for them and we were granted finance to undertake 14 rhythm sessions with 20 children over a period of 7 months. The project was entitled "The Unifying Power of Rhythm for Children Deprived of Parental Care" and the aim was to assist in the social integration of children from the home in Doganovo.

Rhythm was to be the main resource in transforming the negative and aggressive energy of the young people into self-expression and communication with themselves and other people and to achieve positive social results. From a more general point of view our aim was for the children and teenagers in the target group to improve their prospects in life and create opportunities for a more adequate and successful integration in life.

Our more specific aims were to use key themes of active listening, communication, synchronicity and balance to learn the following qualities and skills: co-operation, discipline, participation, sharing and their application in practice.

FIGURE 68
The drums and rhythm give the gift of joy and smiles to children in Doganovo

Below I have presented the results of the project summarized by Katya Tomova, the home's psychologist, based on daily observations and working with the children:

> During the project a number of changes in the behaviour of the participants from the specialized institution were observed. Certain negative elements of institutional care were compensated for. When the children perform, they feel free and communicate freely, both in the group and outside it. After several months work, we noticed increased concentration, a desire for independent work, and the children were visibly more conscientious in performing their daily tasks.
>
> During the therapy none of the following negatives caused by long-term institutional care were observed:
>
> - Stereotypical movements – swaying back and forth and to the side;
> - Thumb sucking;
> - Infant neurosis and facial tics;
> - Stammering in two of the children visibly reduced;
> - Reduction of aggression – children who were considered to be "hooligans" or "difficult children" managed to find a better way of communicating with the others. They were visibly calmer and no deviations in their behaviour were recorded. The level of understanding and friendly relationships increased.
>
> By systematically working with rhythm the children feel stronger, more capable, and see themselves as equal and independent individuals and this led to an increase in their self-esteem. The therapy has also led to an enhanced feeling of wholeness, it has created intimacy between them and especially towards the leaders of the project – Marty and Samuila. The children have created a bond and accepted the leaders in the role of mentors. Giving the children certain tasks to do has been particularly constructive in their work.
>
> By fulfilling these tasks, the children feel independent, confident and capable. We observed one particularly interesting phenomena – children who were considered by the group to be outsiders became leaders and managed to foster an interest amongst the whole group.
>
> One of the children who is slightly underdeveloped and has special educational needs and works with a special teacher, accepted the role of leader

and formed a group of three children who composed a solo together. They called themselves the "Stars" and they presented a solo performance which is constantly being enhanced. They performed it with pride to all our friends and guests of the institution.

In order to objectively record the results of the project a study was made of the levels of aggression and depression amongst the participants. For this purpose tests were carried out before the beginning of the project and after its completion. I can present the results of the study which was carried out by the psychologist, Vesela Ognyanova:

> The first study was carried out at the beginning our joint work, the second at the very end. They demonstrated a reduction in the level of depression: in the beginning the average rate for the group was 28, and at the end – 23 points (fig. 69). This meant that from a level of moderately high depression the therapy led to a level of reduced depression. During the first study nine children were found to have high levels of depression, while in the second study only two children were considered to have high levels of depression (fig. 70 and 71).

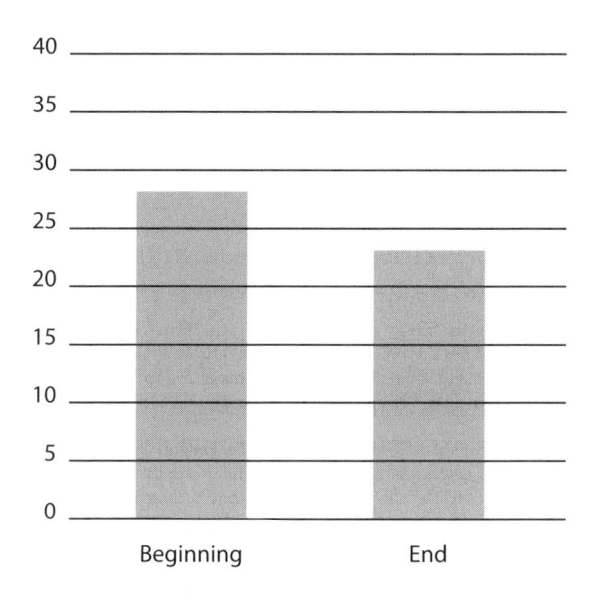

FIGURE 69   **Level of Depression**

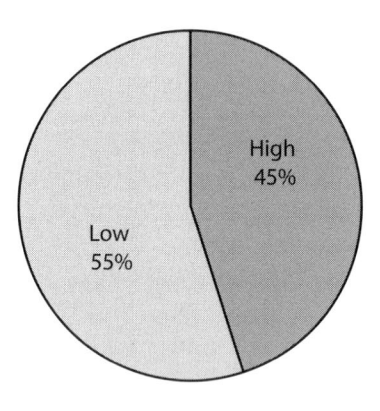

FIGURE 70   Level of Depression - beginning

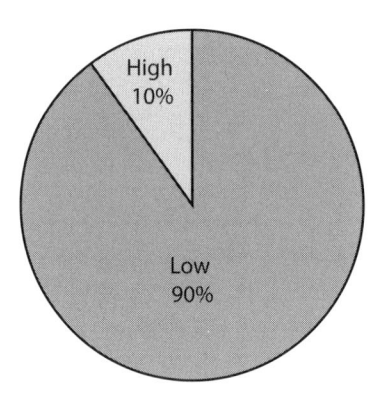

FIGURE 71   Level of Depression - end

We also observed a reduction when studying levels of aggression. To begin with the average score for the group was 5.0 points and during the second test it was 4.7 (fig. 72). During the first test seven children were classed as having a high level of aggression, and during the second – four (fig. 73 and 74). A qualitative analysis of the tests for depression and aggression showed that there was a reduced sense of loneliness and an increase level of cooperation and tolerance.

There was also a reduction of indirect aggression and oppositional behaviour. This means that in the event of problems and conflicts they are willing to share them and clarify the problem, rather than to keep it to themselves and direct their aggression to a weaker person or other object.

In addition to the expected and predicted results of the project, a number of children revealed enviable abilities and talent. Further specialized work will be able to guide them in a direction which will determine their professional career. The "Unifying Power of Rhythm for Children Deprived of Parental Care" project has undoubtedly proven the power of rhythm and the positive results related to its use.

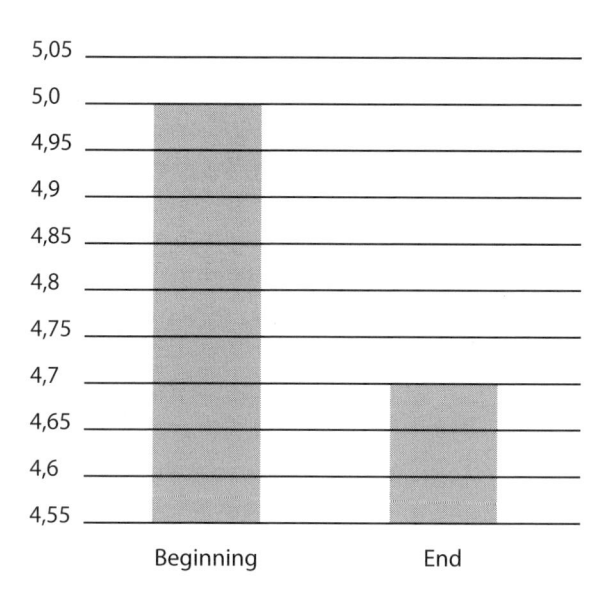

FIGURE 72   **Level of Aggression**

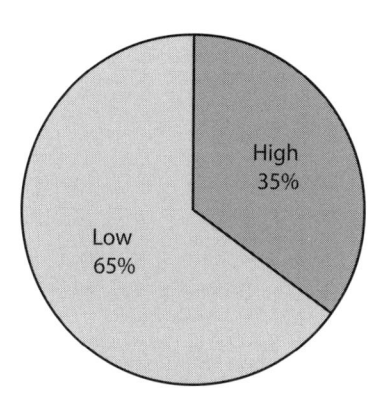

FIGURE 73   **Level of Aggression - beginning**

FIGURE 74   **Level of Aggression - end**

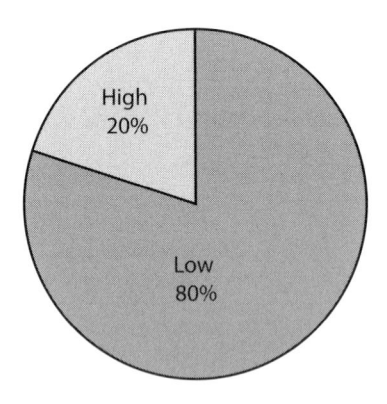

Best of all, over this short period of time the children achieved remarkable success in their studies, discipline and overall development, as a result of having fun accompanied with many smiles and much laughter.

FIFTY-ONE

Rhythmology

The "Rhythmology" programme unites the wisdom of the Vedanta; the philosophy of Hermetism passed down to us over the centuries by the ancient schools of Egypt, Greece and Rome and the mythology of the Mayans.
"Rhythmology" refracts all this knowledge through the contemporary viewpoint and the central idea is the creation of metaphors which can be observed through the eyes of rhythm using the language of percussion instruments.
— MARTIN IVANOV

When I began writing this book, its first title was "Rhythmology". I had written about 60 pages when one day I decided to change direction and began afresh. By this time I had discovered the Virtual Interactive Matrix and the Hermetic formulae but it was all in a very rough form. I developed the idea and desire to create a course with the same name based on rhythm, the Hermetic principles and the mental elements.

My aim was not only to create the opportunity for people to discover their own rhythm and find out more about it, but also to experiment with the Virtual Interactive Matrix. I was faced with the challenge of starting something which was exceptionally different and new even for those people who have some knowledge of the matter.

Now four years later the "Rhythmology" programme is a reality and I can say that it has become very popular and created a lot of interest. At a very basic level participants are introduced to the genesis of rhythm, the Hermetic philosophy and how to use the mental elements. The programme also integrates subjects such as Vibration, Active Listening and Awareness, Communication/Interaction, Synchronicity, Balance/Harmony, which are vitally important for us and determine and dictate our lives.

"Rhythmology" examines all these subjects supported by lecture materials, examples, spontaneous and improvised performance, rhythm and role-playing games, using drums and other percussion instruments.

I cannot deny that many of the tasks and exercises which I present in the programme are aimed at provoking the participants, in the best meaning of the word. This approach allows us to observe and analyze our existence from a different point of view. The multi-functionality and broad applicability of rhythm makes the course effective as therapy, relaxation, toning or just for fun.

FIFTY-TWO

The Rhythmology Experiment

Use your positive vibrations to change reality!

I spent a long time thinking how to give more people the opportunity of completing the Virtual Interactive Matrix. Up until this moment only the participants in the "Rhythmology" programme had access to it. At this stage it was important for me that as many people as possible could hear the rhythm models and record their choices in reference to the mental elements. Although I had a large amount of materials to argue my cause, this would allow me to add more empirical proof about the validity of the Hermetic formulae.

I decided that the best way to do this was on the Internet and this gave birth to the "Rhythmology Experiment". So one fine day the Virtual Interactive Matrix appeared on the Internet.

The aim of the experiment was to analyze the results of the inquiry completed by at least 10,000 people.

This specially prepared questionnaire contains all 27 recordings of rhythm models which have different vibration qualities and character, but have no melody, style and do not evoke popular associations.

I expect to discover specific trends in the perception of the diverse rhythms and to construct associations with specific emotions and feelings aroused by these vibrations. Based on the presumption that we both emit and attract emotions, feelings and thoughts which actively influence our behaviour and respectively the quality of life, the possibility arises that we can discover a new approach to recognizing and mastering emotions, as well as enhancing or reducing the level of transmission.

So, two years after the publication of the matrix, we still have not achieved the desired sample of 10, 000 participants. Nevertheless, people from more than 30 countries have taken part in the experiment. It should be borne in mind that the participants received no specific information about how to complete the matrix, unlike you and the participants in the Rhythmology programme. They just listened to the models and recorded the correspondences with the mental elements.

Despite this fact, the results obtained so far demonstrate certain trends. These trends categorically correspond to the natural emotional pictures which we recreated in the third part of the book. I will not be revealing a great secret if I tell you that the vast majority of the participants in the questionnaire voted for the properties of the mental elements which I used earlier: ANGER (fast tempo, loud dynamics and low pitch), PEACE (slow tempo, soft dynamics and medium pitch) and JOY (fast tempo, soft dynamics, high pitch).

This is everything I can reveal about the "Rhythmology Experiment" at this state before the experiment is complete. For this to happen more quickly, I invite everyone who has read this book and has prepared the Virtual Interactive Matrix to do the same at the following Internet address:

http://libera-institute.com/experiment/?lang=en_us

Thank you in advance!

FIFTY-THREE

Conclusion

What we have done for ourselves alone dies with us; what we have done for others and the world remains and is immortal.
— ALBERT PIKE[32]

We began "Rhythm Alchemy" in a manner worthy of the adventures of Indiana Jones, with the exception that the information presented here recreates real facts. In 1952 Alberto Ruz Lhuillier really did discover the tomb of Pakal and behind the triangular door the "fundamental truth" of rhythm really does exist.

I hope that I have managed to convince you of this. Lhuillier's discovery is also a wonderful metaphor for the journey. The journey which everyone of us has to take in order to search for and discover his or her personal treasury of knowledge. This book is one such journey of searching. This is my adventure and page after page I have ventured forward in my search for my truth.

I recall the moment 16 years ago when I decided to write this book. I had no idea then what tests I would be faced with on my journey and where it would lead to. At that time all my conscious actions were determined by academic music and rhythm was not more than just one component. The fact that music was the meaning of my life created a huge paradox for me – I was incapable of looking beyond the triangular door. My enormous desire to be important and successful in my art had blurred my vision and my consciousness. The more I tried, the more things seemed to be beyond my reach.

Then one day the adventure began when I remembered what the most important thing was. I realized that before we could be creative, capable and competitive professionals, we need, rhythmically to take the next vitally important fresh breath of air. Everything is pointless without it. This was a difficult truth to accept after so many years spent in materialistic intoxication. You like your "*bright dream*",

---

32 Albert Pike (1809 – 1891) – American writer, lawyer, Confederate officer and mason. Pike is the only Confederate military officer to whom a statue stands in the American Capital, Washington.

however uncomfortable you may feel within it. For me this step was tantamount to changing my religion. A long time passed before I could really accept this new reality and then miracles began to occur.

I remembered that it didn't take any effort to breathe in and out rhythmically. It is something I can just do without thinking about it. My entire existence was, after all, conditional upon such an elementary function. The countless vital processes which take place in my body, thanks to the next portion of air, should have been more complex than the profession which I had chosen.

Why then is it sometimes indescribably difficult when I pick up a musical instrument and try to compose a piece of music? Of course, this musical example can be used as an analogy for any profession or type of behaviour. In nature everything takes place effortlessly. Plants, animals, minerals simply exist and waste no superfluous energy in "anxieties or nerves". By understanding this concept I was able to perceive a level of skills in which you can create as effortlessly as you breathe.

As part of this process I focused on studying the way in which nature breathes. I spent a few hours every day playing percussion instruments to the accompaniment of the sounds of nature. I synchronized myself with the pulse of the waves of the sea, rain drops, trickling streams and malevolent thunderstorms. I talked to the buzzing insects, singing birds, barking dogs and croaking frogs. I listened and learnt how nature breathes and I used this knowledge.

In this way my playing, thinking and my attitude towards the world became more natural and more original. The results were not late in coming. The less effort I made, the more things I had dreamed of began to occur. Without doubt the journey requires certain sacrifices, since you need to reject easy thoughts and your comfortable situation, in order to throw yourself into the abyss of the unknown and uncertain.

This is the process of "surrender", not in the meaning of capitulation but surrendering harmful thoughts which devour you like worms. In this struggle it does not matter whether you play an instrument, tighten screws or manage a corporation of five thousand people, since it is a cruel fight with your ego. Final victory depends on the self-sacrifice which you will make. After my initial successes, I decided even more to believe in myself and to take a more powerful step.

I had gradually begun to realize that the creation of the next orchestral composition, conducting thirty musicians who would work like "slaves" to rehearse, then to force the audience to listen and experience pleasure from listening to the same composition, for the pure reason that I wanted to be in the centre of their attention, in order to feed my own personal ego, is not something which made me happy.

What I did was to turn my back on my profession as a composer and musician at the very height of my career. This event preceded my strong desire to help people with various types of problems and difficulties. The only path on this adventure passed through the very place where I had experienced my own problems and resolved them once and for all.

It was very exciting since it was like gathering all your faith and strength to take a step into the abyss – the inimitable experience of the adventure to discover yourself.

Many people ask me: *"Why did you give up music? Why after so many years abroad, studying and teaching in celebrated colleges and so much success, did you take this decision?"*

I have always answered these questions with a short and simple explanation, but now with this book, I am able to provide the complete answer to everyone who is interested. Since I have no intention of describing in detail the difficulties which I have overcome, I shall continue with the positive sides of my journey.

When I regained consciousness after falling from a great height, I patted the dust off my clothes and carried on. Good news was waiting for me. I realized that I had not actually given up music, composition, conducting or performing.

The difference was that I was no longer using my own music but the ANCIENT MUSIC. If my deeply philosophical musical messages required sophisticated and experienced taste to be understood, then ANCIENT MUSIC can be understood by everyone. I could use it to compose, perform and speak to everyone and be understood by everyone without any limitations. I was once invited to be a lector at a TEDX conference in Sofia, Bulgaria.

TED (Technology, Entertainment, Design) is a global set of conferences owned by the private non-profit Sapling Foundation, under the slogan "ideas worth spreading".

The speakers are given a maximum of 18 minutes to present their ideas in the most innovative and engaging ways they can. Past presenters include Bill Clinton, Jane Goodall, Malcolm Gladwell, Al Gore, Gordon Brown, Richard Dawkins, Bill Gates, Bono, Google founders Larry Page and Sergey Brin, and many Nobel Prize winners.

TEDX are independent TED-like events, which can be organized by anyone who obtains a free license from TED, agreeing to follow certain principles.

So as part of the presentation I had set myself the aim of communicating with the audience by rhythm without saying a word.

I went out onto the stage in front of about 700 people and we talked by means of clapping and stamping and so on for about 10 minutes. All this took place in complete synchronicity. If there is a universal language with which we can communicate with each other without preliminary training or no matter what our nationality is, then this is the language of rhythm. With this language I began to communicate with the people and to compose and direct their emotions and feelings.

I realized that my dream of being useful was coming true. The self-sacrifice was worth it.

During the entire time I was thinking about the book which I wanted to write, but I still did not feel ready. I needed to acquire more knowledge. So I read hundreds of books. It is amazing to feel how your vibrations attract exactly that information which you are looking for and which you need. However many times I descended into the depths of ancient knowledge and however powerfully I vibrated at that frequency, the more new avenues and spaces opened up to me.

So, just like in a fairy tale, just at the right time and the right place, the book, page, paragraph I needed, appeared to fill the empty spaces in my theory. I had entered into the high-energy field of synchronicity where my internal reality could find a common ground with the external reality and where the exchange of information was easy and effortless. Something was happening to me – something which Karl Gustav Jung called "synchronous experience".

Gradually this synchronicity overflowed into my direct work. My enormous and sincere desire to work with various public, social, educational, corporate and therapeutic causes by means of rhythm began vibrationally to attract many varied events. I visualized in my mind a group of people with whom I would like to work or places where I would like to go, and sooner or later I received calls and invitations from exactly such organisations and communities.

In this way I took my drums to prisons, psychiatric hospitals, homes for adults, homes for children deprived of parental care, day centres for children with disabilities, oncology clinics and many other places. What was exceptionally useful to me was that I could use my acquired skills in real situations and observe the reactions of the participants with regard to the therapeutic use of music and rhythm.

The experience which I accumulated with a variety of public and social groups, corporate collectives and people with a variety of health problems was invaluable. Thanks to this and my efforts in creating the VIRTUAL INTERACTIVE MATRIX, I managed to increase the level of the sixth sense – INTUITION.

With my enhanced knowledge of vibrations I began to acquire the skill of knowledge without the use of rational processes. The concept of mental elements and their properties is applicable to everything we do: the way we walk, talk, communicate and our body language and gestures in general. The sensation and rec-

CONCLUSION

ognition of a certain vibration model allowed me to predict and expect specific reactions and behaviours.

In this way I managed to construct a correct strategy about how I might be useful both from an individual and group point of view. All this allowed me to construct a unique methodology which is now very successful and popular.

After a number of years of working seriously with rhythm I can see that more and more people in Bulgaria are asking about and are interested in its therapeutic power. I am always receiving letters and calls from people who would like to be trained as rhythm facilitators and therapists. It could be said that in your hands you now have a book which will help you in your training.

"Rhythm Alchemy" is the first and major step towards acquiring the necessary information, knowledge and finding the right direction. Some of you might be asking the question: "*We now know the theory, we have learnt the results, what happens now?*" That, my dear friends, is up to you. Everyone has to walk this path and write their own story and experience. The main element of achieving mastery in mental transmutation is to apply the alchemic processes in a tireless manner.

Do everything you can to accumulate experience and experiment. Look for positive rhythms which will take you to the door of knowledge. Step through the door and find yourself and your happiness!

Twenty years ago I set off in the world to look for happiness. By means of MOTION in TIME and SPACE I completed a full circle and came back to my starting point:

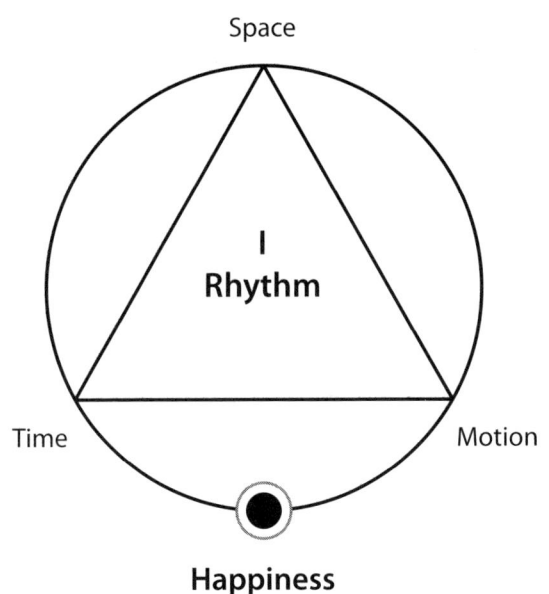

FIGURE 75

Right there at the point from where I had started my journey, I, the person with rhythm inside me, discovered my happiness. I realized that it had always been there and inside me, but the circle which I had to complete was an obligatory condition for finding it.

I am happy because I have managed to open the triangular door and discover my unique gift and talent to be useful to people by doing something which I love with all my heart – RHYTHM!

I wish you all an unforgettable adventure in the world of vibrations.

For up-to-date information

For up-to-date information, additional exercises for mental transmutation and relaxation, courses, programmes, seminars and many other events, please visit: *http://libera-institute.com/*

> The rhythm patterns described in this book can be downloaded in full length as mp3's at the following address: www.findhornpress.com/mp3/rhythm.zip

Illustration Credits

FIGURE 2: Illustration adapted from Maurice Cotterell, *The Supergods*.
FIGURE 3: The British Museum.
FIGURE 5: Photo by Jan Harenburg.
FIGURES 26, 28, 57, 58, 59, 64, 65, 66, 67, 68: Libera Institute Photo Archive.
FIGURES 6, 61, 62, 63: Illustrations adapted from Maurice Cotterell, *The Tutankhamun Prophecies*.
FIGURES 27, 30, 31: Illustrations adapted from Carl Johan Calleman, *The Mayan Calendar* and the *Transformation of Consciousness*.
FIGURES 29: Illustrations from Freidel, Schele and Parker, *Maya Cosmos*.
FIGURE 40: Museum of Antiquities in Turin.

Bibliography

Jose Arguelles: *The Mayan Factor: Path Beyond Technology,* Bear & Company, 1987.

William Arntz; Betty Chasse; Marc Vicente: *What the Bleep Do We Know!?: Discovering the Endless Possibilities for Altering Your Everyday Reality,* Health Communications, Incorporated, 2005.

Robert Bauval: *Secret Chamber: The Quest for the Hall of Records,* Century, 1999.

Robert Bauval and Adrian Gilbert: *The Orion Mystery, Unlocking The Secrets of the Pyramids*, Arrow, 1994.

Ezra Bayda: *Being Zen*, Shambala Publications inc., 2002.

William Bloom: *Psychic Protection*, Piatkus, 2009.

Carl Johan Calleman: T*he Mayan Calendar and The Transformation of Consciousness*, Bear & Company, 2004 & *The Mayan Calendar*, Garev Publishing International, 2001.

Deepak Chopra: *The Book of Secrets*, Rider, 2004.

— *The Seven Spiritual Laws of Success*, Bantam Press, 2006.

— *Power, Freedom, and Grace: Living from the Source of Lasting Happiness*, Amber-Allen Publishing ,US., 2008.

— *The Spontaneous Fulfillment of Desire: Harnessing the Infinite Power of Coincidence,* Harmony, 2004.

Barbara Hand Clow: *The Mayan Code*, Bear & Company, 2007.

Jean Paul Corsetti: *Histoire de l'ésotérisme et des sciences occultes*, Larousse, 2003.

Maurice M. Cotterell: *The Tutankhamun Prophecies*, Headline Book Publishing, 1999.

— *The Supergods*, Thorsons, 1998.

Maurice M. Cotterell and Adrian Gilber: *The Mayan Prophecies*, Element, 1996.

Robert L. Friedman: *The Healing Power of the Drum*, White Cliffs Media, 2000.

Linda Goodman: *Star Signs*, St.Martin's Press, 1988.

Manley Palmer Hall: *The Secret Teachings for All Ages*, Trinity Press, 2011.

Arcobaque Haus & Fernando Malkun: *La Conexion Atlante*, Columbia, 2000. (Film)

Charles William Heckethorne: *The Secret Societies of All Ages and Countries*, Forgotten Books, 2012.

Murry Hope: *The Ancient Wisdom of Atlantis*, Thorsons, 1998.

Kenny Werner: *Effortless Mastery*, Jamey Aebersold Jazz Inc., 1996.

John M. Jenkins: *Maya Cosmogenesis for 2012: The True Meaning of the Maya Calendar End-Date*, Bear and Company, 2012.

Marie Jones: *2013 The End of Days or a New Beginning? Envisioning the World After 2012*, Career Press, 2008.

Frank Jospeh: *Survivors of Atlantis – Their Impact on World Culture*, Bear & Company, 2004.

Hazrat Inayat Khan: *Cosmic Language*, AE. E. Kluwer, 1937.

Lynne MacTaggart: *The Intention Experiment: Use Your Thoughts to Change the World*, Harper Element, 2008.

Neil Powell: *Alchemy: The Ancient Science*, Aldus Books, 1997.

Édouard Schuré: *The Great Initiates, Part 1*, Kessinger Publishing Company, 2003.

Michael Talbot: *The Holographic Universe*, HarperCollins, 1996.

The Three Initiates: *The Kybalion*, CreateSpace Publishing, 2014

Hermes Trismegistus: *The Corpus Hermeticum*, IAP, 2008.

— *The Emerald Tablets of Toth of Atlantis.*

Colin Wilson and Rand Flem-Ath: *The Atlantis Blueprint: Unlocking the Ancient Mysteries of a Long-Lost Civilization,* Sphere, 2001.

Further Findhorn Press Titles

The Alchemy of Voice
by Stewart Pearce

What Does Your Voice Say about You? Your voice is your identity in sound. It is far more than just a means with which to communicate your thoughts and feelings; it is the expression of your integrity and individuality in the world!

Here are straightforward and highly effective techniques Stewart Pearce has used with stars and top businesses for developing vocal skills and using them to their best advantage in all areas of life.
Discover your personal 'signature note'— your unique pitch and resonance of voice that allows you to tune into your whole mind and body and be more appealing and persuasive to others. Use the easy-to-follow exercises to achieve inner balance and harmony, boost confidence, add colour and energy to your self-expression and smooth the way with difficult people and situations.

978-1-84409-194-2

Further Findhorn Press Titles

Hardwired for Heaven
by Joan Cerio

What kind of life do you desire? What do you want to be, to achieve, to become? Your thoughts create your reality. But what creates the thoughts that create that reality? Not your mind; not your brain; not your will…

Your heart is the key to all you wish to create, to all you would be… And *Hardwired to Heaven* is the key that unlocks not only the mysteries of the heart, but its magic as well. Let this engaging, informative and surprising journey into the quantum physics, biology, and metaphysics of consciousness, creative energy, and the heart, introduce you to the sacred coordinate within your heart and show you how you can access its energy to truly live your heart's desire.

978-1-84409-463-9

Further Findhorn Press Titles

Gates of Power
by Nomi Bachar

Gates of Power: Actualize Your True Self is an inspirational, informative, and practical guide for those who are passionate about living up to their potential and maximizing their life. The book is based on the Gates of Power Method created by Nomi Bachar.

The Method is a practical, creative, and deeply spiritual path for self healing and self actualization. It empowers and energizes all seven facets of being: Body, Emotions, Dialogue, Creative Expression, Life Path, Silence, and Knowledge. At the same time, it unifies the three aspects of the Self (Emotional Self, Defensive Self, and Expanded Self), creating inner strength.

978-1-84409-466-0

FINDHORN PRESS

Life-Changing Books

Consult our catalogue online
(with secure order facility) on
www.findhornpress.com

For information on the Findhorn Foundation:
www.findhorn.org